Guidelines

VOL 25 / PART 1 January–April 2009

Edited by **Jeremy Duff and Katharine Dell**

Suggestions for using *Guidelines*

Set aside a regular time and place, if possible, when you can read and pray undisturbed. Before you begin, take time to be still and, if you find it helpful, use the BRF prayer.

In *Guidelines*, the introductory section provides context for the passages or themes to be studied, while the units of comment can be used daily, weekly, or whatever best fits your timetable. You will need a Bible (more than one if you want to compare different translations) as Bible passages are not included. At the end of each week is a 'Guidelines' section, offering further thoughts about, or practical application of what you have been studying.

You may find it helpful to keep a journal to record your thoughts about your study, or to note items for prayer. Another way of using *Guidelines* is to meet with others to discuss the material, either regularly or occasionally.

Occasionally, you may read something in *Guidelines* that you find particularly challenging, even uncomfortable. This is inevitable in a series of notes which draws on a wide spectrum of contributors, and doesn't believe in ducking difficult issues. Indeed, we believe that *Guidelines* readers much prefer thought-provoking material to a bland diet that only confirms what they already think.

If you do disagree with a contributor, you may find it helpful to go through these three steps. First, think about why you feel uncomfortable. Perhaps this is an idea that is new to you, or you are not happy at the way something has been expressed. Or there may be something more substantial—you may feel that the writer is guilty of sweeping generalization, factual error, theological or ethical misjudgment. Second, pray that God would use this disagreement to teach you more about his word and about yourself. Third, think about what you will do as a result of the disagreement. You might resolve to find out more about the issue, or write to the contributor or the editors of *Guidelines*. After all, we aim to be 'doers of the word', not just people who hold opinions about it.

Writers in this issue

Henry Wansbrough OSB is a monk at Ampleforth Abbey in Yorkshire. He is Executive Secretary of the International Commission for Producing an English-Language Lectionary (ICPEL) for the Roman Catholic Church, and runs an international distance-learning theology course. His travels in the past year have taken him to Israel and Australia.

Jonathan T. Pennington is Assistant Professor of New Testament Interpretation at Southern Seminary in Louisville, Kentucky, USA. He holds a PhD in New Testament Studies from the University of St Andrews and has published a number of books, including *Heaven and Earth in the Gospel of Matthew* (Brill, 2007) and the edited volume, *Cosmology and New Testament Theology* (T&T Clark, 2008).

Katharine Dell is Senior Lecturer in the Faculty of Divinity at Cambridge University and Director of Studies in Theology at St Catharine's College. She is also the Old Testament Editor for *Guidelines*, and the author of *Job* in BRF's *People's Bible Commentary* series.

Stuart Murray Williams is an expert in urban mission, church planting and emerging forms of church. He is currently the director of Urban Expression, pioneering urban church planting agency, and the Chair of the UK Anabaptist network.

Alec Gilmore is a Baptist minister, writer and lecturer on biblical themes, former editor of Lutterworth Press and Director, *Feed the Minds*. His most recent book is *A Concise Dictionary of Bible Origins and Interpretation* (T & T Clark/Continuum, 2007).

Rosemary Dymond is Rector of Bedwellty with New Tredegar (Monmouth). Before ordination she worked as a research scientist in Leipzig, developing methods for functional brain imaging using MRI.

John Proctor works for the United Reformed Church, teaching the New Testament to students in Cambridge, and to church groups around Britain. Before that he was a parish minister in Glasgow. John has written *The People's Bible Commentary: Matthew* (BRF, 2001), and Grove booklets on the Gospels.

Further BRF reading for this issue

For more in-depth coverage of some of the passages in these Bible reading notes, we recommend the following titles:

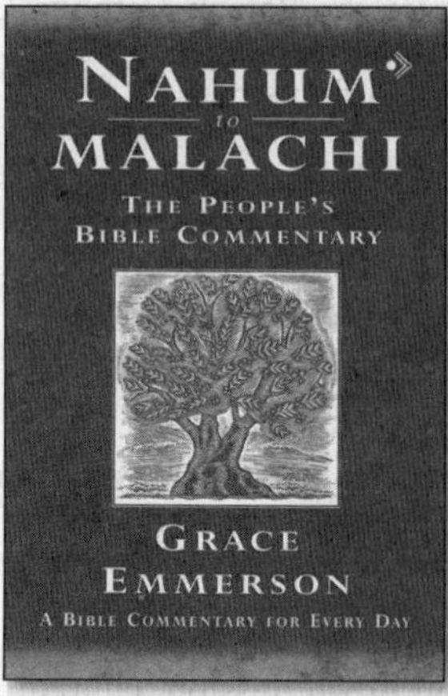

978 1 84101 028 1, £7.99

MATTHEW

THE PEOPLE'S BIBLE COMMENTARY

JOHN PROCTOR

A BIBLE COMMENTARY FOR EVERY DAY

978 1 84101 191 2, £8.99

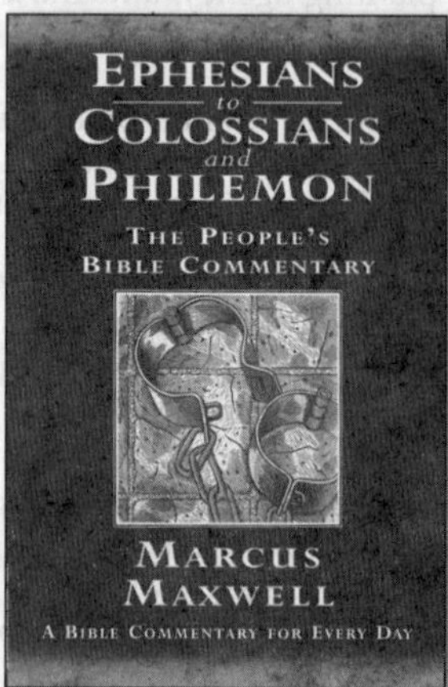

978 1 84101 047 2, £7.99

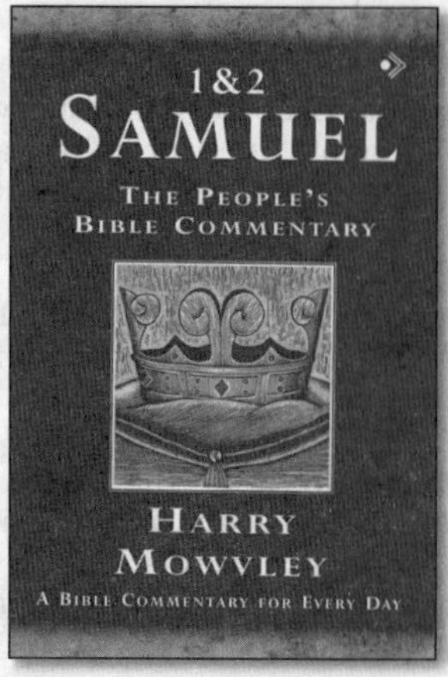

978 1 84101 030 4, £7.99

The Editors write...

Transitions, beginnings and ends, are important for all involved—for communities and for individuals. It is often in those points of change that we are most conscious of both the need for God's guidance and the reality of his presence. Much of this issue of *Guidelines* is taken up with important moments of transition.

From the Old Testament, we look at the character of Ezra as expounded in the book that bears his name and in the book of Nehemiah. Henry Wansbrough brings this character to life for us. We also continue our coverage of the minor prophets with Zechariah, whose strange dreams and visions are elucidated by Alec Gilmore. Both Ezra and Zechariah deal with the exile and its aftermath: how can Judaism navigate the cataclysmic transition that the exile brings? An earlier key transition in the life of Israel is covered by Katharine Dell in the book of 1 Samuel, focusing on the tragic tale of Saul, whose reign as the first king of Israel started with such hope but ended in suicide and despair.

In two different ways we engage with the great events of Jesus' death and resurrection and the change they bring. Jonathan Pennington leads us through the final third of Matthew's Gospel, through Easter to Jesus' commission for his disciples to take his message to the world. Rosie Dymond helps us to look in a deeper way at 'Dying to live'—our relationship with life and death—in the face of Easter and accompanied by the words of some great hymns. That great transition from life to death also features in the letter to the Philippians, written by Paul as he contemplates his own death, and speaks of pressing on to reach the goal. John Proctor is our guide here. Alongside all of this, Stuart Murray Williams presents to us the challenge of urban mission. In past centuries the Church failed to respond well to the transition from rural to urban life. Can we learn from this and do better?

And finally [writes Katharine], a transition for *Guidelines*: 2009 will be my last year as Old Testament editor of *Guidelines* and I am appreciative of all the kind letters that I have received over this time from readers who have enjoyed the contributions. Jeremy Duff is to take over as a joint editor of Old and New Testaments and he assures me that the Old Testament will still occupy a central place in the notes, as has been our tradition over many years of *Guidelines*.

The BRF Prayer

Almighty God,
you have taught us that your word is a lamp for our feet and a light for our path. Help us, and all who prayerfully read your word, to deepen our fellowship with each other through your love. And in so doing may we come to know you more fully, love you more truly, and follow more faithfully in the steps of your son Jesus Christ, who lives and reigns with you and the Holy Spirit, one God for evermore. Amen.

Ezra the Scribe

The period after the return of the Jews from exile is badly documented. We do have, in the early chapters of the book of Ezra, a number of documents relating to the history of the return from exile, but the books of Ezra and Nehemiah are arranged in an order that makes them difficult to interpret. Here, we have selected an order of the events of Ezra's mission that seems to make sense, but this has meant dotting backwards and forwards between the books of Ezra and Nehemiah.

A second problem is the chronology. Reputable scholars differ on whether Ezra and Nehemiah worked together, or—if not—who was first. The position is complicated by doubts over whether the King Artaxerxes mentioned in the text is the first or second Persian king of that name. We will not discuss this matter, but will adopt the solution that follows the biblical text with least emendation: Ezra was sent to Jerusalem by King Artaxerxes I in 458/7BC. Nehemiah was the governor in 445–433 and again possibly in 430BC. Ezra and Nehemiah were not in Jerusalem at the same time, and did not work together.

The work and personality of Ezra are of the greatest importance for understanding the later history of Judaism. He was the first of the scribes (experts in the Law) of whom we have knowledge. He was responsible for the promulgation of the Torah, the Law of Israel, in what must be at least its nearly-final form, promulgating it as the law of the land into which Jesus would come, making it the law under which Jesus would live.

In the second week, we delve also into the book of Nehemiah, where part of the report of Ezra is to be found. The Pentateuch (the first five books of the Bible) underwent a long period of development, beginning with oral tradition of the great stories of the past history of Israel and of early bodies of law. When these had been handed down orally for some centuries, they were collected and shaped into a single story. When Ezra came to promulgate the Law, a recent layer had been added by an author called the Priestly writer, who had written a supplement in which the concerns of the priestly families exiled in Babylon are clearly to be seen. We do not know when the Pentateuch reached its utterly final form, for there were possibly still minor modifications after Ezra's time.

Nevertheless, by the time of Ezra it had reached what would be, to all intents and purposes, its final, written form. This was the Law that would determine Judaism from that point on.

In these readings, we also receive an insight into the spirituality of Ezra and his companions, a spirituality founded on repentance and sorrow for the past sins of Israel. It is very different from the optimism of Isaiah or Malachi, but it is an important element in the later spirituality of Israel, widely seen in the writings of the period.

Quotations are taken from the New Jerusalem Bible.

1 The release of the exiles

Ezra 1:1–8

To understand the story of Ezra, we have to begin a little earlier than Ezra himself, with the decree releasing the Jews from captivity in Babylon. Cyrus the Mede, king of Persia, captured Babylon in 538—bloodlessly, he claims. The rulers of Babylon had attempted to achieve unity in their empire by uprooting the citizens of conquered states and relocating them, so that the subject peoples lost all their national loyalties and characteristics. In this way, the ten northern tribes of Israel had disappeared from history, two centuries before at the hands of the Assyrians. By sharp contrast to this repressive policy of 'ironing out', when Cyrus took the city of Babylon he decreed that all the captive peoples should be returned to their homes, and that the royal resources should be used to help them re-establish their traditional ways of life and worship. By an accident of history, the very decree has been preserved on a cylindrical clay tablet, known as 'The Cyrus Cylinder', the substance of which is given in this biblical passage. As this passage shows, the God of the Jews was known among the Persians as 'the God of heaven', a title always used in the Persian court documents that are included in the Bible. The special treatment the Jews received may be due to assimilation of the Lord by the Persians to their own god, Ahura Mazda.

It was a remarkable stroke of divine providence that the people of

Abraham should in this way be preserved, with their traditions, hopes and loyalties, after half a century of exile, before they had lost their identity. Indeed, in some ways their coherence had been strengthened by a determination to distinguish themselves and mark themselves off from their captors. Their hopes of the unfailing protection of the Lord had been kept alive by the inspiring songs of the prophets such as Second Isaiah, and his proclamation that their time of service was coming to an end. However, many of the Jews had by now settled comfortably in Babylon, so it seems to have been only the most zealous who were prepared to uproot themselves and face the unknown dangers and discomforts of return to the promised land. There remained a large and prosperous Jewish community in Babylon for many centuries, an important guardian of Jewish and rabbinic traditions, destroyed only in the most recent century as a result of the hostilities caused by the foundation of the modern State of Israel.

2 Settling back in Jerusalem

Ezra 3:1–8

We can imagine the privations and difficulties of the journey these families made (Ezra 2:65 gives the suspiciously symmetrical number of 7337 servants, with a total of 42,360 persons), across the 500 kilometres of desert from Babylon to the cultivated land of what is now Jordan. Could this vast medley of men, women and children have made as much progress as 20km a day? How did they get water in this endless flat desert? What about problems from storms and marauders? What happened to sick babies and ailing grandparents? Our passage mentions only the problems of actually arriving in the country—fear of 'the people of the country' (3:3), the members of the population who had not been deported, who would no doubt bitterly resent the return of the exiles to take back the land they themselves had appropriated over the last half-century. We simply do not know how many had remained behind. The two groups were markedly different by now, for 'the people of the country' had not undergone the hardening and welding experiences of the returning Jews, whose religious practices and convictions had developed considerably since they had left Judah for exile.

Our passage describes what must have been an emotional moment as the returned exiles set about renewing the religious practices of their forefathers in the ruins of the temple destroyed by the invaders who had sacked the city so long ago. The book of Lamentations suggests that some sort of liturgical religion had carried on in the ruins of the temple, but the returned exiles say no word about that. They set up a makeshift altar of sacrifice and restarted the regular morning and evening sacrifices. This was only the beginning! The book of Ezra testifies to the dis-hearteningly long struggle to rebuild the temple, delayed by opposition from the local people, who appealed to the Persian governor of the country to prevent progress (ch. 4). Counter-appeals to King Darius in faraway Persia produced a letter of confirmation of the right to rebuild and an order to the local governor to help with supplies to facilitate offerings for his own royal family (6:3–12). Progress was slow, and it needed repeated chiding and encouragement from the prophets Haggai and Zechariah to overcome the depression. The high hopes of the return had long ago been dissipated, and it was a couple of decades before the Passover could be triumphantly and joyfully celebrated in the rebuilt temple in April 515BC (6:19–22).

3 Ezra the scribe (1)

Ezra 7:1–6

Ezra is described as 'a scribe versed in the Law of Moses' (v. 6) or (in the Persian document) 'Secretary [or scribe] of the Law of the God of heaven' (see v. 12). We do not know what his relationship was to Artaxerxes, 'king of kings', or the royal court—whether he was a permanent official, whether he made an appeal to King Artaxerxes or whether King Arta-xerxes headhunted him for a job that he felt needed doing. Ezra is also described (in verse 11) as a priest, and carefully gives his genealogy as far back as Aaron the chief priest (vv. 1–5).

During the exile in Babylon, the Law had become increasingly important. As there was no longer any possibility of liturgical action, no ritual, no temple, no king or royal establishment, the Law was, for the Jews, the only factor of cohesion. So Israel-in-exile developed the way of life that would become and characterize Judaism. It was an immensely important half-century. The book of Deuteronomy was completed, and no doubt some of its regulations were also incorporated into the earlier editions of the Law. It was during this time that the three principal 'boundary markers' of Judaism were developed—observance of sabbath, circumcision and ritual food laws—which served to distinguish the Jews from the other inhabitants of Babylon. These became the basis of the Jewish way of life.

The Law, however, was far wider than this, for it was now that Judaism advanced from henotheism to monotheism. Back in the days of the temple, the central belief was that the Lord was the unique protector of his chosen people, but it was still possible to hold that other nations had their own divine protectors (henotheism). Now, faced at close hand with the full polytheism of Babylon, the exiles were forced to ask themselves whether these too were authentic gods. Their answer was that the Lord is the unique Creator and Lord of the whole universe, and the other 'gods' are nothing (monotheism). The Babylonian gods of sun, moon and stars suffer the ignominy of being stuck in God's heaven as mere time-markers, indicators of seasons for the Lord's festivals (Genesis 1:14). The results of this most significant of all beliefs were incorporated in the theology of the creation stories, which use Babylonian myths and images but in a way totally different from that of the Babylonian stories themselves, expressing a noble theology of monotheism and of the dignity of the human creature—the climax of all creation and God's own representative on earth.

4 Ezra the scribe (2)

Ezra 7:7–10

So Ezra, learned in the Law, will have been not merely a lawyer in the modern sense of the word—an expert in how to behave and obey the rules—but also a theologian, learned in the theology of the Law, its conceptions of God and the divine love of humanity. However, as is the case with all bodies of law, experts were needed to settle priorities when different laws clashed, and Ezra 'had devoted himself to studying the Law of the Lord so as to put into practice and teach its statutes and rulings' (v. 10).

Scribes get such a bad press in the New Testament that it is valuable to look rather more clearly at their task. The bad press derives from their association with the Pharisees. This, in its turn, is the result more of controversy with the Pharisees in the generations after Jesus than of Jesus' own relations with the Pharisees. Jesus seems to have discussed points of law with them using their own methods, though often reaching different conclusions, and they had no part in his execution. However, in the first generations of the Church, the Pharisees spearheaded the opposition to Christianity.

The Pharisees, according to the Jewish historian Josephus, were the strictest party of the Jews, devoted to exact observance of the Law, particularly of its ritual requirements. For this reason they were most in need of expert advice when clashes between laws arose. One case found in the New Testament is that of the farm animal fallen into a pit on the sabbath (Matthew 12:11): some lawyers/scribes ruled that humane treatment of animals dictated that the animal should be hauled out, others that the prohibition of work on the sabbath implied that it could be fed in the pit but not hauled out. In any case, the scrupulous needed a ruling. (Another more laughable case occurred to me once in Jerusalem: one sabbath a man met me in the street, holding out a cigarette and lighter, asking me to light his cigarette for him: it is forbidden to *make* fire on the sabbath, but not to *keep fire burning*.)

In Christian biblical theology, a number of principles are used in deciding which rulings are most important. Is the teaching constant in scripture (the option for the poor, the limitless demand for forgiveness)? Is it dependent on now outdated social conventions (the inferior status of women)? Is it dependent on a fundamental principle of revelation (the infinite value of every human being)? In Judaism as in Christianity, the scribe learned in the Law is still required.

5 Ezra's commission

Ezra 7:11–26

The king's commission to Ezra is framed in exquisitely courteous and diplomatic language, worthy of any royal court, but also implying real respect for 'the God of Jerusalem'. It comprises three elements, first of which is the permission for a party of Jews (not, as we have seen, the first group to return) to go from Babylonia to take up residence in Jerusalem. The king is careful to state that only those who wish to go should do so. Obviously there must have been many who did not want to do so, and perhaps some fear of undue pressure. The money collected 'throughout the province of Babylon' (v. 16) was probably funding for the returnees to help them establish themselves back in the homeland. We are reminded of the pressure on modern Jews to emigrate to Jerusalem, which is often presented as a moral obligation on all Jews.

Secondly, the Jewish Law, the Torah, is made not merely the religious law but the state law throughout the province of Transeuphrates, and is to be taught to those who do not know it (v. 25). Ezra is given the commission to appoint magistrates to administer the Law, and power to impose punishments. This is therefore a real law of the land, spreading to all the inhabitants the observance of the laws evolved for the community in Babylon—a change which will have done nothing to increase the popularity of the returned settlers with those who had not been deported.

Thirdly, Ezra may requisition a considerable sum of money for the temple from the authorities of the province, almost a blank cheque, and all the Temple clergy are to live tax-free (vv. 21–24). This is a handsome gift on the part of the king, and shows real reverence for and cooperation with the religion of the people of this province of his. What were the 'articles' (v. 19) given to Ezra for the ministry of the temple? We might wonder whether they included the objects originally looted from the temple by the conquerors. Were these being returned to their original use?

In any case, this was a far-ranging commission, definitely establishing Judaism as the official constitution of the province of Transeuphrates in the seventh year of Artaxerxes—whether this was the first ruler of that name (that is, in 458BC, 80 years after the return) or the second (that is, in 398BC, a century and a half after the return).

6 The journey to Jerusalem

Ezra 7:27–28; 8:15–31

We now come to Ezra's own report of his expedition, beginning with a fine prayer of thanksgiving for the king's generosity. The intimacy of this prayer suggests that the report was more his own private diary than an official report back to the king. There follows (after the list of the families involved, whose chief interest is the careful linkage of the families to the great figures of Israelite history) the account of preparations for the journey. This has some fascinating features.

Firstly, there was obviously real danger on the route. Ezra is clearly determined that he will not repeat the mistake of kings of Judah before the exile, by invoking secular assistance and so implying that the Lord is unable to protect his own. But he is nevertheless scared—and not without good reason, for piracy on this route was standard, and cities on the trade routes across the Arabian desert, such as Palmyra and Petra, made good money by guaranteeing police escort and protection. So Ezra's preparations are prayer and fasting to recommend himself and his company to the Lord's special care. It must have been with a sigh of relief that he noted, on arrival, that the hand of the Lord had been 'over us and protected us from enemies and surprise attacks on our way' (v. 31).

Secondly, the spirituality displayed by 'the fast to humble ourselves before our God' (v. 21) is typical of post-exilic spirituality. All the Jewish sacred literature of this period shows a deep sense of guilt and shame, a lasting spirit of penance for the sins of their ancestors. Confession of guilt is a repeated feature in the book of Ezra (for example, 9:6–12) and is a special feature of the book of Baruch, the post-exilic psalms (for example, Psalm 51 and such prayers as Tobit 3:2–6.

Thirdly, Ezra is not naive about the honesty of his priestly companions charged with carrying the bullion; they did indeed have a valuable load, for a talent was roughly 60kg. He gives them a little pep talk to start with, reminding them that not only the vessels they are carrying but also they themselves are sacred to the Lord (v. 28). Furthermore, they are carrying other people's gifts. Not content with this, he carefully weighs out the precious metals to ensure that nothing is filched on the journey and checks by further weighing before delivery on arrival.

Guidelines

A prayer:

Lord, grant us the fidelity to your will and your Law which was displayed by these exiles. They were faithful to your call amid all the trials of exile and persecution, amid a society that spurned, mocked and persecuted them as misguided and naive. When we meet mockery, misunderstanding and contempt, enable us to continue firm, calm and welcoming, to show with understanding patience the values that your loving gift of yourself has given to our life.

1 Promulgation of the Law

Nehemiah 7:73b—8:8

The definitive moment of this significant occasion is the promulgation of the Law. Despite being buried in the middle of the book of Nehemiah, it follows logically on from our previous reading about the journey to Jerusalem, for which Ezra had been commissioned to promulgate the Law (see the Introduction for comments on the order of material). The beginning of the seventh month (September/October) was the logical time to initiate the new code, for it was the pre-exilic beginning of the year, after the harvest festivals had brought the old year to a close. The Law thus solemnly promulgated was no doubt the Torah as it then existed—that is, the first five books of the Bible in their nearly-final state. Ezra can hardly have finished reading these books on a single morning, but the note at 8:18 allows him six other mornings, which may well have sufficed.

The manner of reading or proclamation is important. It was no cursory proclamation but the model for all reading of the word of God. The people stand up to receive this gift. Then the reading itself begins with a blessing, and thanksgiving for this great gift. The Law was God's gift of himself to the people, revealing his nature and his covenant with his people, and evoking their response in friendship and love. Their response occurs immediately in the great cry of 'Amen! Amen!' (v. 6). This word is normally the formula for acceptance of an oath as binding on oneself, so the people are joyfully accepting the gift and proclaiming their willingness to observe it.

The reading is further accompanied by prayer—and enthusiastic prayer, so that Ezra has to tell them to restrain their weeping (see v. 9).

Were these tears of penitence or tears of joy? The Torah is always a gift received with joy and gratitude, as anyone will testify who has seen in synagogues the dancing with the scroll of the Law. Obedience to the Law is no burden but a privilege, enabling the faithful to enter into company with the Lord. By revealing the divine prescriptions, it reveals what sort of person the believer must be to enter into company with God and to be part of God's people.

Ezra does not simply read; he also translates and explains (v. 8). Presumably he was reading in Hebrew, the language in which the Law was written, and the fact that he had to translate it implies that there were already many who did not understand Hebrew. Presumably Aramaic, the semitic language of the royal court, had become the normal vernacular. He also explains: this was a commented reading by the scribe/lawyer.

2 The study of the Law

Nehemiah 8:9–18

The first thing to notice about this reading is that suddenly 'His Excellency Nehemiah' has appeared on stage. Nehemiah was sent from the Persian royal court on a separate expedition, and the relative timing of the two expeditions has been a matter of endless dispute between scholars. The name is omitted in the apocryphal book of Esdras I, which is largely parallel to this account; it is tempting to assume, at least for simplicity's sake, that Esdras was the original text, and that Nehemiah had no part in this ceremony.

We begin, then, with Ezra's exhortation to restrain their tears of repentance or of joy, and to celebrate this spiritual event with secular rejoicing and feasting—surely a sound instinct! Notable, however, is the immediate special recommendation of the option for the poor, which runs through the Bible like a golden thread. The people are to give helpings of good cheer to those who have none, and it is confirmed that they do just that (v. 12). One of the strongest points of the Law is that God's own generosity must be shown by his human representatives, created in his image. Adam continues the divine work of creation by naming (finishing the creation of) the beasts and by peopling the earth. The earliest Book of the Covenant (Exodus 20—22) is designed to protect the weak. The Code of Holiness (Leviticus 17—26) resounds with instructions that the Israelite must be generous to the orphan, the widow and the stranger, as God was to them when they were strangers in Egypt. Especially after the exile, this favour of God for the poor becomes evident (Zephaniah 2:3). In the New Testament, Luke especially stresses again and again that Jesus was descended from a poor family, and underlines the duties of the rich to the poor (and the danger of wealth). Jesus himself makes a beeline for the poor, the crippled, the outcast and the sinner.

Another lovely feature of this week's celebration is the study of the Law. Already, on the second day, the heads of families and others gather to study it. This is the beginning of the careful study of the Law which, in some traditions of Judaism, must be continuous: there must always be a group studying the Law. It does not yield all its richness in a moment but requires the meditative and prayerful study which is a tradition both in Judaism and in Christianity.

3 The problem of mixed marriages

Ezra 9:1–12

After the reading and study of the Law, Ezra's dramatic horror at the revelation that some of his men have married the women of 'the people of the country' seems a little melodramatic and staged. The various incidents of his mission are, however, not easy to chart chronologically: this scene need not follow the previous one closely.

Mixed marriages had always been a delicate subject. The patriarchs had sent back to their homeland to get wives for their sons, and had deplored any unions with the locals. This was no doubt simply a custom related to purity of racial stock—a motive that still enters into Ezra's thoughts (v. 2). Much more important, however, was religious contamination, of which there had been plenty ever since Solomon married foreign wives and allowed them to 'sway his heart to other gods' (1 Kings 11:4). Another famous early deviant was King Ahab, who married Jezebel, the daughter of the priest-king of Tyre, and allowed her almost to wipe out the prophets of God (1 Kings 19:10). The sexual shenanigans associated with the 'high places' are continuously denounced by the prophets.

It may well be that, at this time, there was real danger of deviance from the Law being introduced. We have no means of judging whether Ezra was merely being fussy about the form of observance followed by his settlers and neglected by those who had not undergone the traumas and advances of the exile. There was certainly, within Judaism of this period, a somewhat unattractive xenophobia. Perhaps it was the only possible means of maintaining the purity of the tradition and the full observance of devotion to the Lord.

It has frequently been suggested that the passages in the accounts of Israel's arrival in Canaan after the exodus which insist on the destruction of all before them—the *herem* or curse of destruction—were in fact inserted at this time. The situations after the exodus and after the exile were, of course, similar, and the dangers of contamination by the residents of the country were greater in the later case, since the new settlers were of the same racial stock. Refinement in morality, however, makes it difficult for our minds to justify the wholesale slaughter and destruction at the time of the entry into Canaan, even (or especially) in the name of religion. Compulsory divorces are little better and hardly accord with the respect for marriage enjoined by the Ten Commandments, nor with the need to care for the children of such marriages.

4 The obedience of the people

Ezra 10:1–17

This chapter holds a touching combination of principle and practicality: the people assemble, duly contrite, but complain (v. 13) that they cannot stay outside in the torrential rains of the rainy season long enough to settle the matter. (The ninth month is November/December, when the rains can indeed be heavy.) The judges of each individual case are appointed, though it is not clear what the grounds of distinction between different cases were. The regulations of Deuteronomy 7:3–4 are uncompromising: 'You must not intermarry with them… for your son would be seduced from following me into serving other gods.' Perhaps the applications of the law were less draconian than Ezra's initial proclamation suggested, just as the application of the 'curse of destruction' certainly was not absolute at the time of the earlier entry in Canaan.

The manner of the arrangements for judgment of the cases suggests that the community at this time was still a small one, huddled round Jerusalem. The people are given only three days to assemble, and then they all fit in the square in front of the temple. This accords with other scraps of evidence that the post-exilic community remained close to Jerusalem, where they were able to come up to the temple frequently for the various feasts. Otherwise it is difficult to believe that large numbers of people would be able to observe the regulations for thrice-yearly visits to Jerusalem for the pilgrimage festivals, in those days of foot-travel. Our information for this whole period is extremely sparse and does not improve until the Maccabean period, more than a couple of centuries later.

Ezra's prayer is again typical of the post-exilic spirituality of guilt: he speaks of the forbidden marriages as '*adding to* Israel's guilt' (v. 10), a guilt therefore which he sees as already existing. This is a far cry from the optimism of Second Isaiah, writing shortly before the end of the exile: 'Speak to the heart of Jerusalem... that her guilt has been atoned for, that, from the hand of the Lord, she has received double punishment for all her sins' (40:2). It is far also from the optimism of the Third Part of Isaiah, written some time after the return; this sees the nations coming to Jerusalem to draw salvation from it and proclaim the Lord's praises (Isaiah 60:1–11). The final vision of Zechariah also sees the nations coming up to Jerusalem to keep the feast (Zechariah 14).

5 The ceremony of expiation

Nehemiah 9

This ceremony fits no other occasion so well as the conclusion of the 'cleansing' of the mixed marriages. The Law has clearly become the centre of Jewish life. The liturgy is almost sacramental, including long readings from the Law, prolonged confession of sins and concluding with praise to the Lord. This passage is not necessarily culled from Ezra's report, which provided much of the earlier material, and it may well be an anachronistic accommodation to the author's own day. The link of the occasion to the promulgation of the Law is to be deduced from the fact that the Levites listed are those who feature in Ezra's initial promulgation.

The long psalm-like prayer is a survey of Israelite history, and of the Lord's loving care for Israel at every stage, beginning with strong emphasis on the universal Lordship of God, which had been one of the theological advances of the Babylonian exile. At each stage of the history, the extravagant divine generosity is stressed, answered by Israel's grumbling disobedience at every stage. There are two especially attractive features to this prayer—firstly the warmth of devotion expressed to the gift of the Law, sabbath and statutes; these are considered not as restrictions but as signs of the Lord's favour (vv. 13–15). Attractive also is the constant stress on the revelation of God to Moses as 'a forgiving God, gracious and compassionate' (vv. 17, 28, 31). This remained, throughout Israel's history, the dominant picture of God's relations with his people.

The final lines, proclaiming the present slavery of Israel to foreign kings set over them, accords more with the later period, when Israel was forced to submit to her stronger neighbours, Egypt and Syria, each anxious in turn to expand their empire. It might date from the Maccabean period, but it is impossible to date with any accuracy. Penitential liturgy it certainly is, and it has affinity with a number of psalms that could have been used for a penitential liturgy in the post-exilic temple, such as Psalms 74, 79 and 83, all surveys of Israel's repeated disobedience and failure to respond to God's love.

6 The aftermath

Nehemiah 1

After Ezra's promulgation of the Law, all did not go smoothly. In 445BC (and here we have a definite date) the message arrives to Nehemiah, who describes himself as cupbearer to the king (v. 11), that the colony of returned settlers in Jerusalem is in a bad way. Cupbearer was an important job but a risky one. When the king sees his cupbearer looking ill, he is concerned also for himself, for one of the duties of the cupbearer would have been to taste the wine and see whether it was poisoned!

The news centres on the fact that Jerusalem's walls have never been rebuilt, leaving the city open to all kinds of attack and depredation. Nehemiah secures the king's permission to go to Jerusalem with a military escort and timber to rebuild the walls. When he arrives, however, he finds that in the dozen years since Ezra's mission, other troubles have arisen—and continue to do so. The task of rebuilding the walls was bad enough, for there was strong opposition from the local inhabitants who were not of the party of exilic settlers, and so were not considered proper Jews. No doubt contempt on both sides exacerbated the hostility. Particularly a trio named Sanballat, Tobiah and Geshem the Arab (2:19) lead the opposition and challenge Nehemiah with a threat to denounce him to the king as intending to use the rebuilding of the walls as a prelude to rebellion. Despite the opposition, under Nehemiah's energetic leadership the Jews set about rebuilding the walls (archaeology confirms that the building was on a slightly smaller scale than the Davidic or Jebusite walls), a task that was finished in the staggering time of 52 days. However, there had also been an agricultural crisis, in which some Jews had fallen so badly into debt that they had been forced to sell not merely their land but themselves both to foreigners and to fellow Jews.

Nehemiah stayed at least twelve or thirteen years and was appointed high commissioner. In 433 he went back to the royal court, returning to Jerusalem on a second mission at some stage in the next ten years, before Artaxerxes' death in 423. This mission was to settle certain irregularities, including ejecting the previously hostile Tobiah, who had managed to get himself palatial lodgings in the temple precincts. There were also all kinds of other slacknesses, such as failures in the liturgy, trading on the sabbath, and the old crime of intermarriage, which Ezra had only temporarily rectified.

Guidelines

A prayer:

Lord, in the little community around your temple in Jerusalem, you were preparing a faithful remnant, purified by fire, to receive your Son Jesus Christ as man. Grant that we may rely on your help in all our difficulties. With your Son's help and in the strength of his Spirit, enable us to treasure what we have received from our fathers and mothers in the faith, and show us how we can continue to grow and develop, so that we may come ever closer to you and prepare a welcome for your Son when he comes to us in glory.

MATTHEW 21—28

The Gospel of Mark has been famously called a Passion Narrative with an extended introduction. That is, it has been recognized that everything in the second Gospel is leading towards the crucial and cruciform final week of Jesus' life. While this view of Mark is a little overstated, there is much truth in it. In part, the same could be said for the Gospel of Matthew. The story of Jesus finds its ultimate meaning and significance when he enters Jerusalem, is tried, beaten, crucified, and then raised. Each of the Gospels comes hurtling down the hill of history to these essential events. It is appropriate that we spend the next four weeks in Matthew reflecting together on the one week that changed the course of human history.

19–25 JANUARY

---

1 God is coming

Matthew 21:1–17

One interesting difference between the Synoptic Gospels (Matthew, Mark, Luke) and John is that in John's Gospel Jesus is regularly going in and out of Jerusalem. We can trace Jesus' life in John according to his attendance at various holy festivals throughout the year in Jerusalem. In contrast (though not in irreconcilable tension), the Synoptic Gospels do not ever describe for us Jesus' entry into Jerusalem until the final week of his life. This has a great theological point behind it. The Synoptic Gospels reflect a geographical and theological move from the hinterland in the north (especially Galilee) towards Jerusalem where all of Jesus' ministry and life comes to its great climax. Here in Matthew we have now arrived at this point. All of the rest of the book will take place in and around Jerusalem, with the exception of the very final scene where once again Jesus commissions his disciples from a mountain top in Galilee.

Our passage for today describes Jesus' exciting entry through the gates into Jerusalem, his actions in the temple, the resulting conflict with his enemies, and his return outside the gates to the outskirts of Bethphage for the night. In this one day momentous things occur. There is so much of theological weight in this passage that we must inevitably only scratch the surface. Let me make just a couple of observations.

Firstly, note that the identity of Jesus as the Son of David is emphasized here, even as it was in the first chapter of Matthew. We may recall that Matthew 1:1 identifies Jesus as the Son of David, and the following genealogy reiterates the same. Throughout the Gospel this title has also appeared frequently. Now here at the end of Jesus' life this truth is underscored once again. The significance of this truth about Jesus' identity is made clear in today's text. The hope for One to come from the line of David (as king) is the hope for God himself to come to restore, rescue and redeem Israel, to establish God's reign on earth. This is the great hope and expectation that the Jewish people learned from the Old Testament prophets. The crowds rightly perceive that Jesus is this One. And this theme frames our whole passage for today. Notice that the chief priests and scribes understand the implications of the people's words and they are indignant that Jesus does not stop them (v. 15). He responds by quoting Scripture and affirming the people's recognition of him.

Secondly, note that Jesus shows himself to be not only the Davidic King, but also a prophet. The function of the Old Testament prophets was to speak words and perform symbolic actions that communicated to Israel God's warnings and promises. Jesus does no less here. The significance of Jerusalem is not only that it is the city of David, but also that it is the location of Yahweh's temple, the place on earth where God meets with his people. Jesus' prophetic symbolic action against the temple communicated very clearly to the people of Jerusalem: God is coming and stands in judgment over the reigning establishment in Jerusalem and the temple. It is on this bold and foreboding note that the first day of the last week ends.

2 The true temple and true faith

Matthew 21:18–27

Although it may not be immediately apparent, our passage for today overlaps very much with the previous one, particularly Jesus' cleansing of the temple. This story of Jesus' cursing of the fig tree seems very odd, even capricious. Why does Jesus respond so violently to this fig tree, especially if, as many scholars have suggested, this wasn't even the season when fig trees should be bearing fruit? And how does Jesus' teaching about the power of faith relate to this anti-agricultural event?

The answers come from understanding that verses 18–22 are intimately related and together make one important theological point. The fig tree in our story clearly represents Jerusalem and any Jews who oppose Jesus. The withering of the tree is another metaphorical image of God's judgment on unbelieving Israel and its leaders, even as the cleansing of the temple was. (And recall the regular theme of fruit-bearing in Matthew: see 3:8–10; 7:16–20; 12:33.) Mark (11:11–14) makes the connection between the fig tree and the temple even clearer, but we are meant to discern it here in Matthew as well. Jesus then goes on to speak about the necessity and power of faith. A moment's reflection on Matthew reminds us that faith—and particularly faith in Jesus—has been an important theme throughout, especially in Jesus' conflict with the religious leaders. In other words, throughout Matthew we have been hearing the message that now in Christ the people of God are defined not by ethnic descent (being a Jew) but by faith in Christ. Thus, this passage combines these twin truths of judgment on unbelieving Israel and emphasis on the need for faith in Christ. In a very real sense the temple is being replaced by faith as the way to approach God rightly.

Verses 23–27 also overlap with yesterday's passage in that we see once again that the Jewish leadership mostly opposed Jesus. As Jesus enters the temple once again (v. 23) he is challenged to explain his claims to prophetic and kingly authority. But Jesus knows their hearts and knows that their questioning is not sincere, so he refuses to answer them directly. These verses set up an open conflict between Jesus and the Jewish leaders that will consume the next couple of chapters in Matthew, resulting, of course, in his ultimate death.

3 The true Son

Matthew 21:28—22:14

Our passage begins with the question from Jesus, 'What do you think?' This signals that he is continuing the discussion of his conflict with the religious leaders and that he has now turned on the offensive, as it were, and is directing questions to his opponents. Today's passage is a longer one, but it is important to read this section together because it is an intentional unit. Jesus' teaching here focuses on a series of three related parables, all using the metaphor of a son.

The first two of these three 'son' parables are sandwiched together and make the same point. In the parable of the two sons a contrast of peoples is set forth. The first son fails to do as he is commanded but then repents and does right. The second son feigns obedience with his words but then disobeys. If there is any doubt about who these two sons represent Jesus makes it clear in verse 31; the contrast is between the 'sinners' of the world and the Jewish leaders who are supposedly 'righteous'. The statement about the leaders' rejection by God is as bold and explicit as we have yet seen from Jesus.

The second parable (21:33–46) is even more directed and aggressive. Here, leaning heavily on a similar parable of judgment from Isaiah 5, Jesus paints a picture of the evil of the Jewish leaders in rejecting him. This will result in God's rejection of them and God's exalting of the rejected One.

The third parable (22:1–14) is even longer and serves as the climax of this set of three. Here, in addition to the themes of sonship and God's judgment, we also encounter the image of God as king and the provocative picture of the final, eschatological banquet. In fact, this parable with its clear 'end-times' (eschatological) imagery hearkens back to chapter 13 and the parables of the tares and wheat and the dragnet of fish. It also looks forward to the further discussion in chapters 24—25. This parable in particular has some elements that are difficult to decipher, such as what the 'wedding garments' are, but the overall point is clear. There is a day coming when God will judge those who reject his Son.

Thus, all three parables focus on the theme of the failure of many in Israel to accept the coming of God's Son in Jesus. By using a series of 'son' parables here Jesus answers the leaders' questions back in 21:23. Jesus' authority comes from the fact that he is the Son—Son of David, Son of Man, and Son of God.

4 True wisdom

Matthew 22:15–46

Throughout Matthew we have witnessed conflict between Jesus and the religious leaders. This reaches a head in chapter 12 where the leaders (especially the Pharisees and scribes) decidedly reject Jesus, accusing him of demon possession. After this, Jesus continues to have debates and disagreements with the Jewish leaders, but it is no longer a dialogue. Instead, in every case the leaders are seeking to discredit Jesus. Here in chapter 22 is their last and most concentrated effort to do the same.

After Jesus' series of three parables of judgment (21:28—22:14), the Pharisees and Sadducees respond with their own string of three questions intended to entrap Jesus. For the first question the Pharisees (Jesus' number one opponents) join forces with some followers of Herod and present to Jesus one of the stickiest and trickiest questions of the day, a question that sits at the intersection of politics and religion (22:15–22). As in our own day, being questioned on a difficult religious and political question in public is usually a no-win situation. For a first-century Jew living under the oppression of Rome, the stakes were even higher. Jesus' answer, 'Give to Caesar what is Caesar's and to God what is God's', is memorable, brilliant and wise. And it is a 'stumper' for the Pharisees.

The Sadducees, another religious group, based mostly in Jerusalem, ask another difficult question, this one verging on the absurd (22:23–28). Their question is similar to philosophical debates about whether an all-powerful God could make a rock larger than he himself can lift. There is no good answer. Jesus responds with another brilliant and insightful argument straight from the Scriptures.

For the third question (22:34–40) it is notable that these two groups, the Pharisees and Sadducees, gather together to oppose Jesus. It is notable because these two groups were generally in conflict and disagreement themselves. The perceived threat of Jesus' power and influence is such that they must act together. And yet again Jesus answers their theological question with great acumen. Once again, even Jesus' enemies would have to acknowledge the wisdom of Jesus' answer.

If this were where our passage ended we would have grounds to stand in awe at Jesus' insight and shrewdness. But in the final verses (22:41–46) Jesus turns on his enemies and asks his own stumping question: a long-standing theological dilemma about the relationship of the Messiah to David. This question not only serves to show Jesus' superior wisdom (notice the response in verse 46) but also focuses our attention once again on who Jesus is. He is the Christ, the Messiah, the Son of David, now returning to Jerusalem.

5 True leadership

Matthew 23:1–12

This is not the first time that Jesus has had strong words to say against the scribes and the Pharisees. In fact, it is the scribes and Pharisees who seem to be Jesus' main interlocutors during his earthly ministry; he rarely has conflict with any other segment of the Jewish population. Why is this? It is probably because the Pharisees and scribes were actually the closest to the truth in doctrine and practice. That is, they were the 'conservatives' of the day who cared very much about the commands of God and the importance of pious traditions. This aligns them at many points *with* Jesus as compared to other groups within Judaism such as the Sadducees, Herodians and the Sanhedrin. And yet it is a sociological reality that we tend to level the harshest criticisms and critiques at those who are close to us in many ways, but deviate in others.

So what is the content of Jesus' critique of the scribes and Pharisees here? It is found in essence in verse 3: preaching one thing and practising another. We call this hypocrisy, and we have seen Jesus condemn this habit of heart earlier in Matthew (especially 6:1–21). Jesus shows respect for what the Pharisees are trying to do in upholding God's commands (v. 2), but he ultimately rejects them because they have a fundamental heart defect: they lack compassion for others (binding them with burdens and being unwilling to help, v. 4) and they perform pious acts for the praise of people rather than the praise of God (recall again 6:1–21).

Instead, Jesus teaches his way: leaders should be servants of others, not burden-binders (v. 11) and the great ones should be the most humble, not exalting themselves (v. 12). These twin truths and heart habits are both counter-cultural and counter-intuitive, but they are perfectly aligned with the kingdom of heaven.

One practical difficulty of this passage is the question of whether Jesus is here condemning all use of titles such as Teacher or Master or even Father (vv. 8–10). In short, the answer seems to be that the problem is not with the titles per se, but with the great potential temptation associated with all titles, namely that the title-bearer will come to think highly of himself/herself and begin to revel in the title rather than in service to others. I do think it is appropriate that my students call me 'Dr Pennington' rather than 'Jonathan' in class, but I must always guard my heart from finding pleasure or pride in such a title; I must strive to consider these brothers and sisters of mine as more important than myself, even as the Lord of glory did himself in becoming man (Philippians 2:1–11).

6 The Lord is coming

Matthew 23:13–39

This highly structured series of 'woes' on the Pharisees and scribes may seem a bit shocking, especially if our image of Jesus is one wherein he is *only* seen as gentle, compassionate and meek. These things he certainly is—and in abundance—but this does not prevent him from levelling strong rebukes when needed. We cannot perceive from the pages what Jesus' tone of voice was nor his facial expressions, but we can see that he is playing the role of a prophet, both in his pointed exhortations and his tearful lament over the sins of God's people (especially v. 37).

Although these words were addressed in a particular historical situation to Jesus' opponents, there is much we can learn and apply to our own lives from their content. I will mention two in particular. First, notice the profound statement in verse 23. The Pharisees' problem is that when it comes to true righteousness they major on the minors and minor on the majors. That is, they focus on diligently performing certain detailed traditions regarding tithing, while neglecting what Jesus calls the 'weightier' matters of the law. These he defines as 'justice, mercy, and faith'. How might this be true of us? Are there ways in which we are scrupulous about our own 'righteousness'—maybe especially ways in which we think others are failing—while we are blind to the larger and weightier matters of justice for the oppressed, mercy and compassion for the needy, and faith directed towards God?

Secondly, notice the powerful images of verses 25–28. Jesus defines hypocrisy as appearing righteous before others while having corrupt hearts. This outward–inward distinction is true of all of us to some degree, of course; we are flawed and inconsistent people. Yet, more fundamentally, we should ask ourselves whether there is indeed a deep-seated disjunction between our public lives and our private ones. Take our speech, for example. Do we put on a face of kindness and smiles in public but then use our tongues to criticize and destroy those same people or even those in our own family? This kind of dual living is precisely what Jesus is condemning, as does James (1:22–26; 3:1–12).

We must make a final note about how our passage ends (vv. 37–39). We began this week's readings with Jesus' entry into Jerusalem. This was not only a geographic move but a theological one, heading into the final and crucial week of Jesus' life. At that time, the crowds cried out, 'Blessed is he who comes in the name of the Lord', while Jesus' enemies opposed this. Now, here Jesus ends his discourse by drawing us back to the significance and reality of his coming into Jerusalem. Even as we saw in chapter 21, Jerusalem and the Jews are being judged for their faithlessness, and the focal point of this is none other than Jesus himself. The following two chapters will unpack what this future reality looks like.

Guidelines

As we have observed, these three chapters in Matthew are centred geographically and theologically in Jerusalem, framed by the reference in chapter 21 to 'Blessed is he who comes in the name of the Lord.'

In these chapters we have seen a Jesus who is more aggressive and pointed than we have come to expect. In these chapters we have followed his violent overturning of temple furniture at the beginning to his harsh words towards his enemies at the end, with a series of parables of judgment in between. What are we to make of this, especially as we consider the reality of Jesus as our exemplar and we as imitators of him?

At the risk of oversimplification, we may suggest that in Jesus we find the proper balance of the need for both gentleness and strength, of meekness and majesty. There is a time and a season for healing and mercy, and there is a place and time for standing for truth and justice and defending the right. Taken together these seem in tension, but in the right situation the one is appropriate and the other not. Jesus is our model in both.

One key for our application today is to know ourselves well. Some of us tend toward the 'standing for the right' approach, and others of us tend toward the 'meekness and compassion' mindset. Being conscious of our own tendency and being open to acting otherwise is the key toward striking a balance. We should reflectively and prayerfully ponder each situation, asking whether God is calling us to stand boldly or serve quietly. Both are needed realities.

1 When will these things be?

Matthew 24:1–14

This week's readings make up the fifth and final discourse of Jesus' teachings in the Gospel of Matthew. We have already heard from Jesus the Sermon on the Mount (chs. 5—7), the discourse on missionary service (ch. 10), his teaching in parables (ch. 13), and a treatise on the Church (ch. 18). Now, fittingly, we have the final teaching block that emphasizes the future and the 'end times'. There are many memorable images and teachings in this discourse, yet there is also much controversy, especially on how to understand what Jesus is talking about here. 'End times'—or, better, 'eschatological' matters—will always be debated because their very nature requires this. They involve matters in the future and thus are inherently uncertain, and moreover, they use language that is highly metaphorical, symbolic, and suggestive more than concrete.

Our verses for today set up this lengthy eschatological discourse. As we have discussed previously, the narrative has brought us to the climactic last week of Jesus' life, all centred on Jerusalem. This discourse is no exception. In the preceding chapters Jesus has entered Jerusalem, cleansed the temple, and spoken strong words of judgment and lament over the city and her people. Now, in response to his disciples' awe at the glowing beauty of the temple structure, Jesus boldly predicts that even this great temple—the place where heaven touches earth and where God meets with his people—will be destroyed.

The disciples apparently understand that this event will be connected with Jesus' coming as King and the close of the age (v. 3), but this is as far as their understanding goes. One may recall the disciples' similar question after Jesus' resurrection: 'Is now the time you are going to restore the kingdom to Israel?' (Acts 1:6).

We can imagine that the answer the disciples were hoping for was that Jesus was going to inaugurate his reign and rule immediately (including their consequent rule with him, as he said in 19:28–29). But instead, the answer Jesus gives in 24:4–14 is not a happy one. Between then and Jesus' second coming—an unspecified amount of time that is still in process today—will be a time of trial, tribulation and temptation. It is a time of waiting and a time of proclaiming. And this is the situation we still find ourselves in today—proclaiming the gospel of the kingdom, awaiting the close of the age.

2 Let the reader understand

Matthew 24:15–28

The unhappy predictions about the future continue in our passage for today. Along with the disciples we would hope and expect that Jesus' description of the time before his second coming would be positive and peaceful. Instead, his sobering message is that before he returns as reigning King, ungodliness, war, suffering and tribulation will be the marks of this world and will touch our own lives.

The strange reference in verse 15 to the 'abomination of desolation' (a profaning of the temple by a pagan ruler) is very significant for several reasons. First, as Matthew makes clear, we as readers are supposed to be pointed back to the Old Testament book of Daniel. Daniel is one of the latest books of the Old Testament and its vision of God's coming kingdom was very influential on subsequent Judaism and Christianity. In fact, we know that Jesus' own self-designation 'Son of Man' probably reflects Daniel's vision of a coming Messiah (Daniel 7:13). The book of Daniel also informs the New Testament's vision of the end times or eschatology. Matthew's reference to Daniel here helps us see that Jesus is the fulfilment and completion of God's revelation to Daniel.

Another very significant aspect of verse 15 is what it teaches us about how to understand Jesus' teachings here overall. That is, the 'abomination of desolation' is a great example of how the Bible sees multiple events as being related and having multiple fulfilments. The 'abomination' that Daniel spoke of has already occurred once before Jesus' time, during the 2nd century BC. Jesus predicts it happening again, which it did in AD70. And yet Jesus also looks forward to a future fulfilment at his second coming. We can learn from this example that the teachings in chapters 24—25 likewise have an application not only to Jesus' day but also to ours. There is often much debate about which verses in these chapters refer to events from the first century and which events are yet to come. The example of the 'abomination' teaches us that the answer is 'both/and', not 'either/or'. In this way Jesus' teachings here remain amazingly relevant, applying just as much to his first-century hearers as they do to us, and to everyone in between. Let the reader understand!

Today's reader would also benefit from reading Paul's discussion in 2 Thessalonians 2:1–11. This text seems to be speaking (in more straightforward terms) of the same matters that Jesus is speaking of here.

3 Be ready!

Matthew 24:29–51

In the previous passage Jesus spoke of the great trials and tribulations that his followers would face as they await his coming. Today's verses mark a transition as Jesus speaks about the certain and world-changing time of his return. Here Jesus uses vivid language about cataclysmic events in nature and the spiritual realm (24:29–31). These images are very strange to us but were actually well-known stock phrases used in Jesus' day by many Jews to describe the return of God to judge and save the world. Jesus' choice to depict his own second coming with this language shows that he is claiming to be the centre of God's redemptive work and the One through whom history will come to its completion. He is associated intimately with the fulfilment of God's work in the world and the Jewish people's hopes. This has been a theme throughout Matthew and will continue to the end.

After this Jesus proceeds to use a number of more realistic and easily understood illustrations: the blossoming of a fig tree, the days of Noah before the flood, men working in a field and women at a mill, and a master leaving his servants in charge while he is away.

Through this series of illustrations Jesus is presenting three clear and related teachings. Firstly, Jesus is certainly returning again for the judgment and salvation of the world. Secondly, while there may be hints of the time, the exact day of Jesus' return is not known. And thirdly—and most importantly—we must live diligently *now* in light of this *future* reality. The pervasive sense one gets from reading these verses is that their truth is meant to have a real impact on our daily living now. We are to be like the servants whose master is away—faithful, kind, diligent, honest and good stewards—so that when he does return the house will be in order. This is the same thing as saying that we are to live now *on earth* according to the future kingdom *of heaven*.

In fact, the impulse among many to calculate dates and make predictions about Jesus' return is precisely what this passage does *not* encourage. Knowing this precise time is impossible and is unknown even to the Son (24:36). But what can and should be known is how we are to live now in this time of expectant waiting.

4 The ten maidens

Matthew 25:1–13

Here is a striking image that has inspired sermons and sacred art throughout the centuries—the picture of ten virgins waiting for their bridegroom. Five are wise and prepared; five are foolish. Five enter into joy; five are locked out and grieved.

This teaching from Jesus is a parable. He introduces it in just the same way that he has introduced many of his other parables, with the formulaic words, 'the kingdom of heaven is like/will be like this...' (see Matthew 13:31, 33, 44, 45). Indeed, this parable is one of a series of three parables or illustrations that Jesus gives together (24:45–51; 25:1–13; 25:14–30), all of which have the same point: be prepared for the Lord's second coming.

The difficulty of interpreting parables is that we can often get caught up in the details and miss the main point. This parable is a great example of this danger. That is, our tendency when reading a parable in the Bible is to try to make one-to-one connections with elements in the story and elements in our world; we tend to read in an allegorical way, i.e. this equals that. And when we do so, we not only often miss the main point of the parabolic teaching, but we also end up reading things into the text that are not meant to be there. Moreover, this kind of parable reading can also leave us confused.

So, for example, we might first be taken aback by the fact that Jesus compares himself to a bridegroom—clearly his role in this story—who is about to marry ten maidens. (There is nothing in the Greek to suggest that these are 'bridesmaids', as some translations put it in an effort to domesticate the shocking image.) This may seem to us to be presumptuous, un-Christlike, and maybe even chauvinistic! Additionally, what are we to do with the element in the story that when the unprepared virgins ask for oil from the others they are roundly refused? Is this Christian sharing? And when the five maidens do arrive late, why are they not allowed in? Presumably if they were to be married to the bridegroom he would have known them and welcomed them.

These problems with the parable show that this approach for reading will not work. Instead, we need to let the parable be a self-contained story, not pressing the individual elements too far or forcing them to correspond to everyday realities. The point of the parable is clearly stated by Jesus at the end: 'Therefore, be alert, because you don't know either the day or the hour [of Jesus' return]' (25:13).

5 The talents

Matthew 25:14–30

As we observed in the previous passage, this is the third of three related parables (24:45–51; 25:1–13; 25:14–30), all exhorting us to live well now in light of the delay of Jesus' return. We can see that we are to read these three parables together because they deal with similar content and because the first and third are linked together with the same language of the gnashing of teeth, an image of future judgment. All three parables deal with the main character going away and then returning, but the first and third are particularly similar in that they both involve a master going on a journey and the behaviour of his servants while he is gone. Such an analogy works well for the disciples of Christ.

Yet this third parable in the series advances the story even further. Rather than just teaching us that we are to wait patiently and expectantly for Christ's return, this third parable adds the new element of rewards and talents.

The story Jesus tells here develops along typical lines, with three different servants coming before their master in turn to give accounts and be rewarded accordingly. Of course, the striking and disturbing part of the story is the third servant who, from our perspective, may not appear to have done anything overly wrong. Yet his decision not to use the money entrusted to him proves to be a fatal flaw and a failure to live faithfully for his master.

The idea of using one's 'talents' (from the Greek word meaning a unit of money) appropriately is both familiar and easily applicable. What talents—in the form of money, other assets, skills and gifts—do you have? And are you squandering them or using them to invest in the kingdom? We may recall Paul's teaching about the necessity for all the parts of the body of Christ to serve as they are called (1 Corinthians 12 to 14). What part in the body has God gifted you to play? We are living now in a time of waiting for the Master to return. Now is the time to live faithfully with all that we have been given.

6 The sheep and the goats

Matthew 25:31–46

We now come to the final section of the final discourse or teaching block in Matthew. And it is certainly a dramatic and powerful ending. This teaching once again comes to us in the form of a parable, at least in part. The separation of the sheep from the goats is typical agricultural imagery common to the first century. In this way, this parable is like Jesus' many other parables involving common experiences such as sowing seed, catching fish and growing mustard seeds. But unlike Jesus' other parables, this conclusion to the eschatological discourse combines a farming image with an explicit and straightforward picture of the future judgment of the world. The Son of Man appears with his angels, and the reality of entering the Father's kingdom is very explicitly the point.

These concluding verses are interlaced with many other portions of scripture, including earlier sections in Matthew. For example, we may observe that this ending to the fifth discourse is strikingly similar to the ending of the first and third discourses (chs. 5—7 and 13 respectively). Specifically, each of these teaching blocks in Matthew ends with a vision of the future judgment in which all the world will be separated into two groups: two types of building foundations (7:24–27), two types of fish (13:47–50), and two types of animals (25:31–46). This similarity is no accident from the pen of Matthew, and the astute reader is meant to see the emphasized point. These verses are also connected closely with the book of Daniel, and particularly the idea of the Son of Man exercising dominion and authority (especially Daniel 7:13–14).

The point of a future judgment by Christ is clear enough in this passage. The theological question that arises, however, is *upon what basis is this separating judgment made*? An initial reading of the text might lead one to think that the future judgment of all people depends solely on one's philanthropic practices toward fellow humans. That is, visiting the sick and imprisoned and feeding the poor is what enables one to enter the kingdom. While these are certainly good and godly and Christian practices, this view will simply not square with the rest of scripture. Throughout the New Testament, including in Matthew, it is clear that one's relationship with God is on the basis of faith in Jesus Christ; there are no accidental Christians who enter the kingdom by simply doing good deeds.

So what is this text teaching? The answer is twofold. Firstly, this text reflects other Matthean (and New Testament) teaching regarding the outward fruit borne by an inward reality. That is, the ones who produce such good fruit do so because inwardly they have been transformed through Christ (see, for example, 7:15–20; 12:34–35). Secondly, it seems that the 'least of these' in 25:40, 45 are none other than Jesus' disciples. This has been the way that the disciples have been described in many places, including chapters 10 and 18. Thus, the point of this parable is that the nations will be judged on the basis of how they received or rejected Jesus' disciples.

Guidelines

I suppose there are three kinds of people in the world: those who are fascinated by and focused on 'end times' scenarios and teaching; those who are completely ignorant of them; and those who know that the Bible speaks about such matters but are not interested because of knowing too many people in the first category! Certainly the 'end times' has always been a topic of interest and discussion; this is not just a modern phenomenon. Unfortunately, there are many people whose Christian faith is focused almost exclusively on such matters. I say 'unfortunately' because often such ones have a sincere interest in the things of God but have a truncated and misdirected understanding. It is undeniable that the New Testament is thoroughly eschatological or future-focused. As one scholar has put it, to be a Christian is very much to be one whose life is shaped by the hope of God's future. Thus, it is right to think for and hope in God's coming kingdom. After all, this is at the core of the prayer Jesus has taught us to pray: 'Thy kingdom come, thy will be done, on earth as it is in heaven' (Matthew 6:10).

Yet there is a way of studying and thinking about the end times that is more akin to conspiracy theories or science fiction thrillers than to biblical witness. In the scriptures we are given many images and parables about the future but their exact meaning is unclear. We are not able to nor are we meant to be able to nail down specifics of times, places and events concerning the end times.

Instead, the application of eschatological teaching in the Bible is two-fold. Firstly, these teachings are meant not so much to fill our minds with theories but to change our daily living. That is, the point of Jesus' vision of the coming kingdom is to exhort us to live *now* in light of the coming *future*. Because of the certainty of the coming kingdom, we as followers of Christ need to align our lives according to the principles and truths of God's reign. Secondly, these teachings give us great and sure hope. The fallenness of this world—from injustices to illnesses to natural disasters—will one day be set right. God is restoring all of his creation, us included, and this hope is what enables us to endure with faith. Whatever trial or difficulty you face this week, set your heart and hopes on the reality of God's coming kingdom.

1 The trap is set

Matthew 26:1–16

We now enter the final and climactic section of the Gospel. The events of Jesus' suffering, death and resurrection are the focal point of the whole Gospel story and are the apex to which all the narrative has been leading. We have heard Jesus' final teaching discourse, and now what remains is the final step in the working out of God's plan.

We have already heard Jesus tell his disciples about his coming suffering and death (16:21), but now he sets this sad fact in a very particular time frame: in two days' time at the Passover. Immediately following this brief account, Matthew sharply juxtaposes another scene, that of the meeting of the chief priests and elders (vv. 3–5). The mounting opposition of the Jewish establishment to Jesus has come to a head. With the high priest's own involvement and approval, they have decided to kill Jesus and put an end to his teachings and movement.

Then immediately Matthew places before us yet another scene (vv. 6–13). In this well-known story, a woman follower of Jesus shows her love and devotion by sacrificing a flask of very valuable perfume. It is interesting to note the reaction of the disciples. Certainly they felt justified in criticizing this woman's actions. Have they not been taught by Jesus that wealth is not to be squandered but to be used for the glory of God? Have they not been taught that one should lay up treasures in heaven by giving gladly to the poor and needy, not wasting money on elaborate displays? But once again they are mistaken; their understanding is only partial. Jesus shows them that something unique is about to occur: the Son of Man is about to die. This woman has done a good thing and has played a part in a cosmic-sized event that is larger than any principles of financial stewardship.

Judas' decision to betray Jesus follows immediately. We do not know whether this event was the proverbial straw that broke the camel's back for an already disgruntled disciple. The Gospel of John gives us a fuller account, explaining that Judas was angry about this wasted money because he had been pilfering the money box (John 12:6). Regardless, we see that the story that began this chapter comes full circle. Jesus will be handed over and killed and Judas has provided the chief priests with exactly the kind of help they need to take hold of Jesus without causing a riot. They need an inside man.

2 The new Passover

Matthew 26:17–29

It is hard to imagine a more theologically dense passage of scripture. We have here not only the record of a key moment in Jesus' life, but also the culmination of many historical and theological truths from the Old Testament. Additionally, this event is the fount of the Lord's Supper celebration, a central focus in the church's weekly gatherings from then until now.

The theme of betrayal continues in this passage and Judas once again makes an appearance. This talk of Jesus' betrayal casts a dark and ominous tone over the whole scene. It reminds us of the coming darkness in the story. The disciples understandably respond with sorrow and assertions that they are not the one. We can imagine how shocked and fearful Judas must have been when Jesus announced so plainly that he knew one of them was to betray him.

The words that follow in verses 26–29 are some of the most important in scripture. It is no accident that Jesus' ministry and life come to their climax at the feast of the Passover, the single most important festival in Jewish life. Its importance lies in the fact that it is the celebration of the most important event in Israel's history, the exodus. Through the exodus, God saved his people from bondage, revealed himself to them, made a covenant with them, provided for their needs, and led them to the promised land of their inheritance. It is not difficult to see how Jesus himself fulfils and extends all these realities, and this is precisely what Matthew wants us to understand. In this new Passover feast—transformed now into the Lord's Supper or Eucharist—the ultimate deliverance from bondage occurs, the bondage of our own sins. Thus, through the new covenant established in Jesus' blood we find forgiveness, release and new life. The bread and the wine symbolize God's provision, and we are led into the promised land, the place of God's kingdom. And we may note that there is a future focus in Jesus' words (v. 29). Our regular celebration of the new Passover feast looks forward to the day when we will once again be with our Lord in table fellowship.

We may also observe that this institution of the Lord's Supper has ties with many other scriptural events and realities. Jesus' feedings of the multitudes already anticipated this new exodus pictured in the Lord's Supper. Jesus also spoke of a coming messianic banquet in the kingdom. The Lord's Supper anticipates this. And all this, of course, looks back to the covenant God gave through Moses, including the sprinkling of blood for the forgiveness of sins. It serves to heighten our awareness of the depth and gravity of this one short evening—an evening that proves to be a culminating point in history. As we partake in the Lord's table now, let us do so mindful of all that God has done, while also looking forward with great hope.

3 The night of betrayal

Matthew 26:30–56

The Lord's Supper ends with the singing of a psalm, almost certainly from Psalms 113—118 which were used in the Passover celebration. We also once again see a reference to the Mount of Olives. Mountains have played an important part throughout Matthew, including being the place of Jesus' temptation, the place of the Sermon on the Mount, the mount of transfiguration, and the site of the eschatological discourse. The whole Gospel will also end with Jesus giving instructions from a mountain in Galilee. Indeed, this is anticipated in Jesus' statement about going before them into Galilee (v. 32).

As the Passover night descends, we see several pictures of the failure of the disciples. Firstly, Jesus tells them plainly that they will all fall away from him, which is precisely what happens at the end of verse 56. Beloved Peter, whose zeal is both his greatest strength and weakness, is the ultimate example of the disciples' failure. Peter has been the one who has been the first to understand, the first to confess, the first to get out of the boat. But even Peter, the apparent leader of the disciples, will deny his master three times! Secondly, we see the disciples' failure in that when Jesus asks them to pray and watch, they can do nothing but fall asleep. And finally, we also see the brash ignorance of the disciples through the model of one who tries to defend Jesus by the sword. Notice Jesus' response: I do not need the strength of twelve disciples; I could have twelve legions of angels if need be (v. 53).

In addition to the failure of the disciples, the other key theme in this text is the sovereignty of God. Throughout, Jesus emphasizes that these events are not chaotic or out of control, but all has happened to fulfil the words of scripture. Additionally, in Jesus' own prayer we see a beautiful picture of what it means to trust in God's sovereignty. Jesus understandably expresses his own desire to be delivered from this coming trial and suffering, but he concludes with these precious words, 'not my will but your will be done' (v. 42). Therein we find the model of true faith: trust in God's power and goodness, and a heart willing to submit to the same.

4 Two interviews

Matthew 26:57–75

Matthew has provided us with two related scenes, both of which are interviews in which one is questioned intensely. The juxtaposition of Jesus' and Peter's interviews—and especially their different outcomes—is striking and memorable. We can see how the two scenes are interwoven by the reference to Peter in verse 58. This bold and beloved disciple was told by Jesus that he would deny his Lord. However, despite his protestations, Peter fled the garden of Gethsemane along with everyone. Now Peter has returned, following Jesus from a distance, hoping to remain incognito, but needing to know the outcome of this night's tragic events. While the proceedings of Jesus' trial are going on inside, Peter's northern accent gives him away around the night fire. Poor Peter. Try as he might to be faithful, his fear of being found out and arrested proves too much. He not only denies knowing Jesus three times, but he does so with vehement oaths, breaking one of the specific commands Jesus has taught in the Sermon on the Mount (5:33–37). Once again Peter serves as the model disciple—the model of eagerness and following, and the model of failure. We, like Peter, can never sustain our best intentions. Ultimately we all choose self-protection. But gladly, we see God's grace through Peter's story. He is restored (shown most explicitly through the threefold story in John 21) and becomes a great leader in the early church.

While these events are going on, Jesus is enduring a mockery of a trial with silence and composure. The only charge that is eventually confirmed by witnesses is Jesus' claim to destroy the temple and rebuild it. Of course, this itself is a misunderstanding of Jesus' words. But most notably, the high priest moves beyond this charge to the greater issue—Jesus' identity. The question is whether Jesus is truly the Christ, the Son of God. To this Jesus finally responds, but not with a simple denial or affirmation. Instead, Jesus raises the ante of the discussion even more. He quotes from a crucial Old Testament text, Daniel 7:13, which was widely understood as a reference to the power and majesty of God's Son. This is enough to call forth claims of blasphemy, and Jesus' fate is sealed with the Jewish leadership. So, in contrast to Peter's failure and denial, Jesus stands firm and continues in the will of God laid out for him.

5 Judas' end

Matthew 27:1–10

The first half of chapter 27 consists of two intertwined stories: Jesus' trial before Pilate and Judas' end. Matthew introduces the first story in verses 1–2, and we'll return to that story in tomorrow's reading. For today, we learn of the death of Judas. There are several observations to be made about Matthew's account of this sad story.

Firstly, notice how Matthew has woven together the trials of Jesus (before the Jews and before Pilate) with the accounts of two particular disciples, Peter and Judas. In the one case, as we have seen, Peter fails in denying Jesus, yet he will eventually be restored. In the other case, Judas also fails and repents, though his end is less positive. We do not know why Judas repented of his betrayal. Did he think that Jesus would not be killed? Did he think only that the Jews would stop Jesus but not kill him? Did he suddenly change his opinion about Jesus' innocence? We do not know the nature of Judas' repentance, but Christian tradition has understood Judas as the opposite model from Peter—of an ultimately failed disciple.

Secondly, we may notice the great irony in the actions of the Jewish leaders. We can imagine how warm and welcoming they were to Judas when he slipped into their meeting and agreed to betray Jesus. Their true hearts are seen in their callous response to Judas afterwards. The irony is particularly found in their discussion about what to do with the returned blood money. They are scrupulous about not allowing such money to be returned into the temple treasury, but are completely unconcerned that they themselves have betrayed innocent blood. This is precisely the kind of gnat-straining, camel-swallowing hypocrisy that Jesus has condemned.

And thirdly, we may observe that once again Matthew returns to a key theme that he has developed throughout the book—that all the events surrounding Jesus are the fulfilment of the prophecies from God. In this case the meaning and nuances are quite deep. To explain it in a simplified way, we have here a quote from Zechariah 11:13, which Matthew cites as being from Jeremiah. This technique is used so that the astute reader will read together the two similar passages of Zechariah 11:13 and Jeremiah 19:1–13. When these texts are read together and understood in light of the events in Matthew we can see that there is a subtle but powerful point being made. The message is that God is judging the Jewish leaders (and Judas) for not being good shepherds but instead for shedding the innocent blood of the God-sent prophet, Jesus.

So what appears to be simply a tragic tale about Judas is actually a profoundly powerful message about God's judgment on unbelief.

6 'His blood be upon us...'

Matthew 27:11–26

The Jewish leadership, including the high priest, had already determined that because of the charge of blasphemy Jesus must be put to death. The fact that they must now deliver him over to the Roman proconsul is very telling. Pilate's involvement reminds us of the pervasiveness of the Roman imperial context in first-century Judaism and Christianity. The fact that the Jews must involve Pilate—whom they hate as a foreign tyrant—in their own theological affairs reveals their status as an oppressed people. As I often remind my students, when reading the New Testament one must always remember that the flag of

SPQR (*Senatus Populusque Romanus*) flies over every page.

We have in this story yet another series of dialogues, with the scenes shifting between Pilate's interviews with Jesus and his public discourse with the Jewish leaders and populace. At the literary level we may also notice that Matthew has crafted these scenes to show their connection with the previous dialogue between Judas and the Jewish leaders. Both of these events use the language of 'innocent blood' and the declaration 'See to it yourself' (27:4, 24). The irony is that the same language used between Judas and the Jewish leaders is now reversed and spoken with a different effect between Pilate and the Jewish leaders.

Jesus is once again reviled and mistreated and once again he responds with few words and no retaliation. But just as in his trial before the Jewish leadership, one thing becomes clear: Jesus' identity is that of the Christ. It will not do to think he was crucified for simply being a political or theological revolutionary. The core matter is whether he is the Christ, the Son of the living God, or not. This was the issue for the Jews. And even though he did not believe it himself, Pilate had enough sense also to realize that Jesus' identity was the issue. He continually refers to Jesus as the Christ to jab at his own enemies, the Jewish leadership.

We may make one final and grievous observation. Note the sad irony in verse 25. The Jewish leadership and their riled-up crowd declare concerning Jesus: 'His blood be on us and on our children!' Indeed, in their rejection of Jesus as the Christ, they did bring upon themselves the guilt of shedding innocent blood. Yet at the same time, what they needed was in fact the other sense of this double-meaning language. They needed—as do we—the blood of this innocent man to cover us and be upon us.

Guidelines

The whole story is slowing down to a grinding pace so that these world-changing events can be fully understood and appreciated. We have seen this week many scenes of dialogue between various parties. We have seen various individuals conduct themselves in various ways, sometimes with harsh words, sometimes with great regret afterwards, sometimes with oaths and violent language. But through all the dialogues Jesus has stood with composure and for the most part, in silence. Unlike the previous 25 chapters in Matthew where Jesus has been speaking and preaching and teaching with great boldness and authority, now here he is quiet.

Jesus' response of humility and grace even when being wrongly accused and attacked becomes an important model for the first Christians and for us. Jesus exemplifies the very beatitudes he had taught in turning the other cheek, not returning evil for evil, and non-retaliation, and this was not lost on his followers. We know of at least one way in which Jesus' example here was applied in the early church. In Peter's first epistle he reflects on Jesus' response and uses this as the basis for exhorting Christians to submit to others with humility and trust in God (1 Peter 2:18—3:7). Even as Jesus had no guile, did not revile, and did not threaten, so too should we live in our relationship with others. All of this is possible for us in the same way it was for Jesus, by trusting in the God who judges rightly (1 Peter 2:22–23). That is, by trusting God's sovereignty and ultimate justice. This is what frees us up from having always to defend our own honour and name and the urge to visit vengeance on our enemies.

Instead, may we all learn from Jesus' actions that the way to relate to one another is indeed counter-intuitive and counter-cultural. Through trusting in God we may walk in the way of humility toward one another. Try it out this week. Return to the Beatitudes (5:3–12) and Jesus' model, and follow in his footsteps. This is what it means to be a disciple.

1 Irony in his death

Matthew 27:27–44

The judicial show is over and Jesus is now delivered into the hands of the Roman execution squad. Even as the Jewish leaders had mocked and abused Jesus (26:67–68), so too do the soldiers. But they are much more cruel. In addition to inflicting physical pain they subject Jesus to humiliating dishonour, dressing him up as a mock king and bowing before him. Yet he remains silent.

Throughout this sad and dark story we may notice many deep ironies. For example, the speech of the soldiers and other witnesses is full of language that is meant for mocking but is profoundly true. Of course,

Jesus truly is the King of the Jews, worthy to be dressed in royal robes and knelt before (even as he was truly a prophet: 26:68). The placard nailed above his head is meant by the Romans to signal a warning to any revolutionaries who might attempt to oppose the mighty Roman Empire, but again it speaks the truth about Jesus' kingship. Others mock him for claiming to destroy the temple and raise it in three days. This is precisely what will happen with the temple of his body (cf. John 2:21). The Jewish leaders ironically ridicule Jesus because 'he saved others but cannot save himself' (27:42). Again this is true in a way that they did not perceive: through choosing *not* to save himself he creates the way for others to be saved. We may also notice the ironic fact that none of Jesus' disciples are to be found when Jesus is in need of someone to take up his cross and follow (cf. 10:38; 16:24). Instead of Simon Peter another Simon is pressed into the service of following Jesus and taking up his cross. Finally, Jesus refuses the wine cup of the soldiers because he has already resolved to drink the cup that God has ordained for him (26:39).

We may also observe about this passage that while there are none of the typical Matthean fulfilment quotations ('this happened to fulfil the scriptures…'), this text is rifled through with many strong allusions to the Old Testament scriptures, especially Psalms 22 and 69, and Lamentations. The knowledgeable reader gets the sense that, again, all of these events are happening as part of God's master plan of grace, of life through death, of deliverance through condemnation. As R.T. France has observed, 'The ultimate explanation of the cross is neither Jewish hostility nor Roman injustice, but the declared purpose of God.'

2 Darkness at noon

Matthew 27:45–54

In typical Matthean style, many bits of data concerning Jesus' death are packed tightly together in these brief but weighty verses. We learn of many remarkable events that accompanied the moment of Jesus' death, including daytime darkness, an earthquake, the tearing of the temple veil, the rising of many saints, and the declaration of God's sonship by a centurion. Together these all communicate that the death of Jesus is an unnatural, cosmic and theological incident.

Also typical of Matthew's style, his language is both eschatological and apocalyptic. We mean by 'apocalyptic' that Matthew describes these events with images that communicate more than the literal sense of the words and that speak of a radical disruption in time and nature. We mean by 'eschatological' that Matthew wants us to realize that these events are harbingers of the end of history.

Getting more specific, we may note several of the theological points Matthew wants us to understand. First, the noontime darkness probably recalls the darkness of the primeval beginning of creation. In light of Matthew's many other connections with the book of Genesis, we may observe that Jesus' death is described in a way that speaks of the cosmic disruption that results from the death of God's Son. Related to this, the darkness also connects to the prophetic hope of the Day of the Lord, the beginning of the new age or new creation (see Amos 8:9–10). This darkness also contrasts with the light of the bright star at Jesus' birth and the blinding light of Jesus' transfiguration. Both the stories of Jesus' birth (chs. 1—2) and his transfiguration (ch. 17) have many conceptual and verbal parallels with his death.

The tearing of the temple veil at Jesus' death also makes many theological points. It speaks of judgment upon the Jewish leadership that has opposed Jesus and ultimately arranged his death. It is also a vivid picture of the truth that through Jesus' death the barrier of separation between God and humanity has been torn down. God himself now dwells with his people. No separate priesthood is now needed and no temple rituals are required. Intimacy with God is found through responding to Christ in faith. This is part of the theology of Emmanuel found throughout the book (cf. 1:23; 28:20).

There is much more of importance that could be said about these verses. What cannot be missed is the fact that Jesus' death was a historical fact with great theological meaning. As in all of scripture, these two realities are deeply intertwined. We are meant to read this passage with ears attuned to both.

3 Two requests

Matthew 27:55–66

The great hopes for the Messiah's coming are gone. The one who taught with such authority, healed the multitudes, and even raised the dead is now cold and lifeless. Our short passage for today consists of the interim time between Jesus' death and resurrection. Of course, for those involved in these events they did not know that they were in an interim time. Despite Jesus' many predictions of his death and resurrection, it seems that both Jesus' followers and opponents thought that this was the end of Jesus' story. Our Holy Saturday was for them only another sabbath. We may make a number of observations about these events.

Firstly, note that the disciples of Jesus have been conspicuously absent from every scene since the arrest in the garden of Gethsemane. Only Peter has made a brief appearance right after Jesus' arrest, but his role was one of denier. But we learn in verses 55–56 that at Jesus' crucifixion many of the women who had followed Jesus are watching (and weeping) from afar. All have fled, but now some of the disciples begin timidly to creep back onto the scene. These women will also follow Jesus' body to his rock-hewn tomb.

Secondly, we may observe that Pilate also reappears as a player in these events. He is the focus of two very different requests. A rich Jewish man, Joseph, is granted an audience to request the body of Jesus. We learn from Luke that this Joseph was actually a member of the Jewish council and had not consented to Jesus' condemnation (23:50–51). Pilate probably thinks the request to be of little import and agrees. He is probably a bit surprised and annoyed when the next day he is again approached about the body of Jesus. This time he agrees to let the Jews place a guard at the tomb.

This passage is one of preparation. The mention of the women followers, the laying of Jesus in the tomb, and the Jewish leaders' fear about the disappearance of the body are all elements that lay the groundwork for the world-changing events in chapter 28.

4 Ghosts don't have feet

Matthew 28:1–10

These ten verses describe the single most important event in all of history. This is no small claim, I realize. But if the Bible is accurate and Christianity is true, then this lofty claim is undeniable. This is because the resurrection of Jesus from the dead effects a change in humanity and creation itself. Now humanity's greatest enemy, death, has been defeated, and creation itself, fallen and twisted, is being remade. Jesus' resurrection is the first fruits of the green renewing of all that God has made. As J.R.R. Tolkien describes it, the death of Jesus is the ultimate 'eucatastrophe'; it is a tragedy that hides a beautiful good. We see the consummation and completion of this eucatastrophe in the resurrection, and the good ('eu') part is emphasized.

A few observations are in order. Firstly, note that just as at Jesus' death, an earthquake accompanies his rising from death. These two cataclysmic events are bookended with a shaking of the earth itself. Secondly, we may observe that it is again the women who first learn of Jesus' resurrection and indeed meet him. This is because, unlike the rest of the disciples, they have followed Joseph to the tomb and have continued to go there since. Thirdly, it is worth noting that much emphasis is put here on Galilee. Jesus has told his disciples to meet him there and now he reiterates the same. This will prove important in the final scene of the Gospel. Fourthly, ghosts don't have feet. This vivid notion is probably what lies behind the odd detail found in verse 9, that they 'took hold of his feet'. Widespread in the ancient world and in many cultures today was the belief that spirits or ghosts have no feet. The unexpected detail given here emphasizes the bodily resurrection of Jesus.

Finally, we may observe the two very different responses that these events evoke. The earthquake, the appearance of the glorious angel and the greeting of Jesus result in all the human participants falling down on their faces with fear. For the unbelieving guards the result is only fear, producing terror (28:4). But for those who believed, this fear is mixed with incredible and indelible joy and worship. Notice the beautiful words in verse 8: 'they departed quickly from the tomb *with fear and great joy*'. The same is true today. All of humanity may be divided into two groups depending on how they respond to the resurrection of Jesus. Only those who believe can face life and death with true joy.

5 False report

Matthew 28:11–15

From the epicentre of the empty tomb run two different groups of people. We saw in yesterday's passage that the two Marys run to tell the disciples about Jesus' resurrection. Verse 11 of our text for today informs us that some of the guards who also witnessed the earthquake, angel and empty tomb run in a different direction—to inform the chief priests of all that has taken place. We do not know exactly what they said nor how they were received by the Jewish leaders, but we can imagine it was not a happy meeting. And after taking counsel together, the chief priests once again try to solve the dilemma of Jesus by paying someone off. First it was Judas and now it is the guards.

This story goes back to the events of 27:62–66. The Jewish leaders knew Jesus had predicted his own resurrection and feared that the disciples would steal the body to support this false claim, hence the posting of the guards. Now, in light of these remarkable and inexplicable events they decide to propagate this same story. We can see from verse 15 that at the time of Matthew's writing this theory as to the mystery of Jesus was still widespread. In this the chief priests were successful, at least in part. Those who would not believe had a ready-made answer for the Christians' claims of resurrection.

It is primarily to refute this claim that Matthew has included this part of the story. We may also see that from the beginnings of the Church the real, physical resurrection of Jesus mattered. That is, neither Matthew nor any other early Christian could be content to speak of Jesus' resurrection as if it were merely a metaphor for hope or a 'spiritual' reality divorced from facts. No, to put it as the apostle Paul does, if the resurrection of Jesus is not real then we are to be the most pitied among men, and all is for nought; we remain in our sins and our faith is useless (1 Corinthians 15:12–19). Such is the weight and hope of the resurrection of Jesus. And so, for Matthew and for us, its veracity is worth defending.

6 A word to us

Matthew 28:16–20

We have finally reached the last words of Matthew's Gospel. And just as one's 'last will and testament' is important and lasting, so too are these final instructions from Jesus. This short passage is packed full of Old Testament allusions (especially verse 18: see Genesis 1:26, 28; Daniel 7:13–14; 2 Chronicles 36:23) and connections with previous teachings in Matthew. It is fitting that Matthew concludes with such a highly concentrated text. In fact, one scholar has called these verses the central station through which many of the lines in Matthew converge. For example, we may observe that, like many people before, the disciples now bow down and worship Jesus. We also note that this meeting takes place in Galilee and on a mountain. Both of these sites have been important in Matthew, communicating the ideas of Gentile inclusion ('Galilee of the Gentiles', 4:13–17) and the spiritual significance of a mountain (for example, recall the third temptation of Christ, the place of the Sermon on the Mount, and the transfiguration). The command to go to 'all the nations' also speaks of the Gentile-inclusive nature of the gospel, which is certainly one of Matthew's great concerns. Additionally, we should not be surprised to see in these verses mention of Jesus' authority and the emphasis placed on making disciples. These have both been important themes earlier in the book. Another important theme that is found throughout Matthew also finds mention here—the theme of heaven and earth, a phrase that has appeared many times and is very theologically weighty. Also, the 'I am with you' language itself is pluriform in meaning: it is the divine name revealed to Israel ('I Am'); it hearkens back to the same in 14:27; and it forms a bookend with 1:23, emphasizing God's abiding presence. In these ways and others Matthew uses these final verses to remind us of some of the most important aspects of his Gospel account.

These final verses in Matthew are extremely well known and have had a formative impact on hundreds of thousands of missionaries throughout the centuries. These words of Jesus have often flown as a banner over the work of foreign missions. But they are not just verses for those called to such service. They are the 'great commission' for all Christians. They give the Church the vision for what our calling has been and continues to be throughout the ages: to go to all the peoples of the world (including those in our own neighbourhoods) and proclaim, teach, and make disciples. This work is to continue throughout all generations until Jesus' promised return. Thus, these words are not just a fitting conclusion to this beautiful Gospel, but are a direct word from God to us today. They serve as a lasting word to us about how to orient our lives, priorities and hearts.

Guidelines

For me it has been a wonderful and edifying experience to read and reflect upon Matthew with you over the last year. I hope and pray the same is true for you. Here at the end of our study let me suggest to you what I think are two key theological truths that run throughout this entire Gospel. First, Matthew wants us to understand that *the end of the ages has dawned in Jesus Christ*. Throughout the book we have been hearing about the future end of the ages when God's saving work will be complete. We have also seen time and again that Jesus is the consummation of all of God's dealings with Israel, from Genesis through the prophets. Countless times we have read that such and such happened 'to fulfil what God had spoken…' The significance of this for us is that you and I are living in the final stage of history. The end has begun. As Paul says, we are the ones 'upon whom the end of the ages has come' (1 Corinthians 10:11). If this is true then it is a call for us to orient our lives now towards God's coming kingdom. The teachings of Jesus all throughout this book serve as the blueprint for the kind of Godward, kingdom-focused living to which Jesus calls his followers. And because this is truly the 'end times' there is a needed sense of urgency and importance to this call.

Secondly, Matthew wants us to understand that *the eschatological people of God are defined anew*. One of the main teachings that Matthew has emphasized is that God's dealings with humanity have now definitively moved beyond their previous Jewish orientation. This is not to say that Israel's history is unimportant or that the Jews are rejected, but that the promise to Abraham has now been fulfilled in Jesus, the son of Abraham. This promise is that God will make for himself a people from *every* tongue, tribe and nation, no longer based on (Jewish) ethnicity. Now there is neither Jew nor Greek (Galatians 3:28). Thus, in this final stage of history the people of God are now defined as *all* of those who respond to Christ with faith. The implications for us are great. First, we may stand in awe and thankfulness that God has allowed us to enter the stream of his saving work in the world. Regardless of our backgrounds or pedigree God has welcomed us to hear his gospel message. Secondly, as the great commission makes clear, our call as Christians is to spread to all peoples the message of God's coming kingdom in Christ. It is with a call to this universal and unending task that we end our study of the wonderful Gospel of Matthew. May God make his face shine upon you.

FURTHER READING

The resources on Matthew are manifold. Among the many good commentaries on Matthew, the reader will especially benefit from the works of R.T. France. His shorter commentary is in the Tyndale New Testament Commentary series published by IVP. He has also written a larger, more recent volume in the New International Commentary on the NT (NICNT) series, published by Eerdmans.

1 Samuel

The book of 1 Samuel stands in partnership with 2 Samuel, and both books are regarded as containing the history of Israel, her leaders and her fortunes. We might question the use of the word 'history', in that this is theological history, events being interpreted always with the hindsight of faith. It is also a literary construction—the piecing together of a number of stories—and hence narrative history rather than factual presentation. It forms a part of a longer history that runs from Joshua through Judges into the Samuels and then on into 1 and 2 Kings. This history has been termed by scholars 'Deuteronomistic' as it shows thematic similarities with the book of Deuteronomy and the 'Deuteronomic worldview', which has influenced major parts of the Old Testament.

The Deuteronomic historians drew the whole history together in the latter days of the monarchy, leading up to the exile. They had the benefit of hindsight and they also had many sources of information in front of them. They linked the history with dates and editing notes and the occasional long speech placed in the mouth of a significant person. Otherwise, the stories are self-contained and probably come from a time earlier than that of the redactors. Some may have circulated in oral tradition, perhaps some of them from the actual time of the events they purport to relate.

1 Samuel is dominated by three great men: Samuel, Saul and David. In fact, it can be regarded as a 'Saul sandwich', with Samuel preceding him and leading up to the climax of Israel's demand for a king, and David following, the one who would receive God's favour and take on the kingship in a permanent way. In between comes the narrative about Saul, the first king of Israel, who was to fail and lose the throne. The monarchical experiment was not straightforward in Israel; nor was the transition from judges and priests (such as Eli at Shiloh) to prophetic leaders (as embodied in Samuel), to kings (Saul and David).

Another point of interest is the women in this story. We are first introduced to the mother of Samuel, Hannah, whose prayer for a son is heard and who in turn dedicates that son to the Lord. We also come across a woman in labour in chapter 4, who in her dying breaths manages to name her son with a theological statement.

The version of the Bible we will use is the New Revised Standard Version.

Samuel

1 Barrenness to birth

1 Samuel 1:1–20

We are introduced to Elkanah and his two wives, Hannah and Peninnah. The latter had borne children, while Hannah was barren, and it is possible that Elkanah took a second wife when the first failed to provide him with an heir. It is stressed that Elkanah loved Hannah, giving her a double portion of the sacrifice (v. 5; see Leviticus 6:14–18). It is also stressed how irritating Peninnah was to Hannah, since she had no difficulty conceiving—which reminds us of the situation between Sarah and Hagar, Rachel and Leah (Genesis 16:4; 30:1).

We are also introduced to the northern shrine of Shiloh (18 miles north of Jerusalem), which is the centre of attention in these narratives. Shiloh was home to the ark of the covenant, and its prominence here betrays a time when Jerusalem was not at the centre of Israelite life. This appears to be a personal pilgrimage by Elkanah and his wives, as distinct from the festivals at which male Israelites only were bound to attend.

The sacrifice to 'Yahweh of hosts' (v. 3: the first mention of this divine title in the Bible) is an annual one and every year Hannah gets upset at her lot—for to bear children was *the* sign of blessing for any Israelite woman of the time. We first meet Eli the priest in verse 9, although it is his good-for-nothing sons Hophni and Phinehas who are introduced first (v. 3; see 2:12–17). When Hannah speaks her vow, watched by the priest Eli, swearing to dedicate her first child to the Lord, we are reminded of the Nazirite vow imposed upon Samson's mother and upon Samson himself in Judges 13, another barrenness-to-birth story. Eli's curious mistake, interpreting Hannah's moving lips as a sign of drunkenness, leads him to bless her, and this cheers her up so that, having abstained from food, she now eats and drinks. Hannah must have made such promises in previous years, hoping for a child from the Lord, but perhaps what makes the difference this time is the mediation of Eli the priest. On her return home, Hannah duly conceives and bears a son, calling him Samuel: an important female role in the naming of the child emerges here (v. 20).

2 Hannah's prayer

1 Samuel 1:24—2:10

Returning to the same scene a number of years later (probably when the boy was three), Hannah fulfils her vow and hands the child over to Eli. We then read a piece of poetry which is ostensibly Hannah's prayer, but which is likely to have come from elsewhere in Israelite tradition and been placed, suitably, in her mouth. The link to her situation comes in verse 5b, with the reference to a barren woman bearing seven children, although the other side of the coin is also expressed—that too many children might be less satisfying. The reference to enemies and arrogant talk (vv. 1, 3) could also apply to her conflicts with Peninnah.

The prayer is a hymn to Yahweh, beginning with a triumphal note about overcoming enemies. The names given to God, such as 'Holy One', 'Rock' and 'God of knowledge', all suggest his incomparability, the theme of the second half of the hymn. Yahweh's ability to change fortunes is stressed: not only the power to change barrenness to birth, but also to kill and bring to life, make some people poor and others rich, bring some low and lift others up, so that the poor sit with princes. He is seen to be on the side of the underdog, the poor—ultimately his own faithful ones (vv. 8–9). Verse 10b has echoes of Baal, god of thunder, which suggests that Yahweh is taking over this role (cf. Psalm 29).

The ending, which blesses the king, is odd because kingship was unknown in Israel at the time of Hannah: it arose in her son Samuel's time. This strongly suggests a different original context for the prayer—a nationalistic one, stressing the king at the centre of national life and winning wars in Yahweh's name. This passage therefore must originate from later in Israel's life and have been placed in Hannah's mouth by an editor, perhaps by one concerned to stress the benefits of kingship. It may have come from a time of national victory and been regularly used in the ritual life of the nation.

3 Samuel's call

1 Samuel 3

The dramatic effect of this story is heightened by the repetition, three times, of the call of God, mistaken by the young Samuel as a call from Eli. On the third occasion, Eli realizes that it is God's call and Samuel responds appropriately (with a proper liturgical response), as Eli has instructed him. It is a harsh message that God has for Eli and his house: his sons have caused the end of the lineage by their blaspheming and Eli's lack of restraint of them.

It is interesting that Samuel was lying in the temple at Shiloh where the ark was situated (v. 3). We might wonder if he was guarding it. This verse forms a link with the 'ark narrative' that follows in chapters 4—6.

Our passage ends with the statement that Samuel was 'a trustworthy prophet of the Lord' (v. 20). This was a time of transition from priest to prophet in the leadership of Israel. Samuel carries out ritual functions for the priest Eli at the start of the chapter, but by the end he is described as 'a trustworthy prophet' (v. 20). Scholars have variously interpreted this incident as a prophetic call narrative (v. 1: 'the word of the Lord' indicating a revelatory word of God to a prophet) or as an auditory dream theophany (v. 1 refers to visions) or as a first prophetic experience (v. 7 indicates that Samuel had not previously received a word from the Lord and, indeed, that he did not yet 'know' him, perhaps indicating that their special relationship had not yet commenced). If it is a prophetic call narrative, it lacks the usual commissioning elements, unless the indictment of Eli's house is that commission. The aspect of theophany may be linked to the presence of the ark of the covenant, which was meant to evoke the divine presence.

It is perhaps significant that Eli calls Samuel 'my son' (vv. 6, 16), thus suggesting that he takes the place of Eli's own miscreant offspring. In verses 17–18, having invoked an oath lest Samuel hide God's message from him, Eli recognizes God's purpose in ending the priesthood and beginning a new phase of leadership in Israel with the prophet Samuel.

4 The death of Eli

1 Samuel 4:12–22

The ark narrative begins at the start of chapter 4 and seems to be a self-contained unit running through to the end of chapter 6. The story of Eli continues, although that of Samuel doesn't, and the fortunes of his family are bound up with the story of the ark. The ark of the covenant contained the two tablets of the Law and was the symbol of God's presence, of especial significance in early Israel before the building of the Jerusalem temple. It was thought to bring victory in battle if carried with the advancing army.

At the start of our passage, a messenger comes to tell the elderly Eli, still at Shiloh, that his sons have died in battle and the ark of the covenant has been captured by the Philistines. We need to remember that Eli is blind (v. 15) and so would not have seen the messenger's torn clothes and the earth on his head, indicating his arrival from the battlefield. Tension is built up in the passage by the messenger's not coming straight to Eli with the news (cf. the messengers in Job 1:13–19, who relate the calamities in succession).

It is the news of the capture of the ark that seems to be the final tragedy for Eli, rather than the death of his sons, and he falls back and breaks his neck. He is aligned with the judges of Israel in verse 18, probably by the Deuteronomic redactor who edited the whole of the history. Interestingly, his death is counterbalanced by a new birth (albeit premature, brought on by the shock of the news): a son for his daughter-in-law, now the widow of Phinehas. Such are her labour pains that she too is on the verge of death, but she is able to name the child. This is significant, as the naming of a child was often the occasion for a woman to make a rare political or theological statement, and she does so here. She names the child Ichabod, meaning 'The glory has departed from Israel', in reference to the ark of the covenant (the 'glory' being the sign of God's presence), but also in memory of the child's father and grandfather who have died on the very day of the child's birth.

5 The powerful ark

1 Samuel 5

The Philistines capture the ark of the covenant but they do not realize its power. The Philistines were the chief enemies of Israel throughout the period of the judges (compare the Samson cycle in Judges 13—16) and they hoped by its capture to harness its power. However, this plan works against them. They place the ark in the house of the Philistine god, Dagon (a fertility deity), in Ashdod, a major Philistine city. The first indication of the ark's destructive power where enemies are concerned is that Dagon's statue falls down, not once but twice. The first fall seems to indicate Dagon's prostration in front of Israel's God; the second, with the head and hands of the image broken off, his defeat. Interestingly, verse 5 gives an explanation of a custom at the time of writing. Here we have an older story explaining modern custom: the priests of Dagon do not step on the threshold of the god's house because that was where the severed hands of Dagon were found.

This part of the narrative is clearly a story of conflict between gods, with the Lord pitching his strength against the worthless idol, Dagon. The next stage of the story is a kind of variation on the plagues in Egypt before the exodus, the people being afflicted with 'tumours'. These were probably inflamed swellings of the lymph glands, as in the bubonic plague (see the reference to 'mice that ravage the land' in 6:5, in conjunction with further reference to the tumours, which may indicate a plague carried by mice). The people of Ashdod realize at that point that they cannot keep the ark and so send it to Gath, another Philistine city. However, when tumours are again sent, it is moved to Ekron, a third Philistine location. In panic the people of Ekron want rid of the ark before it kills the entire population: word has clearly got around! There is a clever literary intensification of the afflictions as each town is mentioned in turn. In the next chapter, the ark is returned to Beth-shemesh in Israel, along with the Philistines' guilt offerings, although even that is not a suitable final resting place.

6 Israel demands a king

1 Samuel 8

Samuel's sons, like Eli's, pervert justice, and this is given as the reason for the gathering of the elders of Israel to demand a king. There are no worthy men to succeed these great figures, Samuel the prophet and Eli the priest. Although God tells Samuel to 'listen to the voice of the people', their demand for a king is presented as a slight on God's own kingship (compare Gideon's refusal to 'rule' over the people, believing that it would be a slight on God's rule: Judges 8:22–23) and as part of a predictable pattern of disobedience on Israel's part, dating back to the exodus (v. 8, probably the Deuteronomic redactor's addition).

Samuel's list of the kinds of sins that a king might commit (vv. 11–17) makes up the main body of the chapter, and it may well be based on an actual list of misdeeds of one of the kings, possibly Solomon. The people are warned that he will need a large administration and army: all the sons of Israel will be working for him in some capacity or other. He will also insist on the best produce and lifestyle, he will demand a tithe from the people, and he will want slaves and domestic animals: in essence, he will plunder people and land to furnish his own lifestyle. Samuel (speaking on behalf of God) makes it clear that the people will regret it (v. 18).

Scholars have suggested that this passage, with its negative attitude towards kingship, is the product of hindsight on the part of the Deuteronomic redactors, who were writing long years after the demise of kingship. The catalogue of misdeeds, if not the redactors' own words, might have been a pre-existent list which was used by them.

The people, looking at other nations that did have kings—including the Canaanite nation whose land they inhabited—wish to emulate them. Samuel intercedes with God on the people's behalf and God, surprisingly, seems to give in, thus highlighting the tension in this passage between the rejection of kingship on one hand and its acceptance on the other. This is the opening for the Saul narrative, which begins in chapter 9 and introduces the man who is to be the first ill-fated king of Israel. The ambivalence about kingship in chapter 8 may owe something to the story that is to follow.

Guidelines

In the part of the narrative concerning Samuel, God is very much in charge of the action. Whether he is calling a prophet, condemning a priestly line, countering idols and Israel's enemies or considering the request for a king, God is all-powerful, effecting his purpose through chosen individuals and progressing the history of Israel. It is made clear that insolent opposition to God leads to judgment. Samuel himself is an example of one of God's true disciples, who obeys God's word and consults him in prayer, one dedicated to God by his mother from the very start.

This story of leadership and dedication to God marks the beginning of the prophetic era in Israel, an era that takes over from that of the judges and of the powerful priests at sanctuaries. This cycle of stories might lead us, too, to reflect on the way God works in our own lives. It might help us to see his hand in events. It might also reaffirm the need to trust in him rather than necessarily seeking our own path. Israel's demand for a king is presented as an example of just such a self-seeking on Israel's part, one that will turn out to be a mixed blessing.

The story of Samuel himself is one of discipleship and leadership. Are we, too, ready to hear the word of God and convey it in our own lives? We might respond that we are not of the same status as these great leaders of Israel's past. However, God works through great and small, through the powerful and through the weak. The story of the birth of Ichabod demonstrates a theological message coming out of a situation of powerlessness—of premature birth, the death of mother, father and grandfather and the removal of the most sacred object Israel had, the ark of the Lord.

Saul

1 Saul is chosen

1 Samuel 9:15—10:8

Samuel is forewarned by God that his chosen ruler (note that he does not use the language of kingship here) will be in the vicinity 'tomorrow' (v. 16), and when Samuel sees Saul, God confirms that he is the one. Saul is looking for a seer and finds Samuel. The terms 'seer' and 'prophet' seem to be virtually interchangeable at this point in time. It is somewhat ironic that the whole reason for Saul's presence in the land of Zuph is the loss of his father's donkeys. This gives a comic incongruity to the story—that Saul is looking for donkeys and ends up being anointed king.

Samuel is able to confirm, quelling Saul's initial worries, that the donkeys have been found. He then states cryptically that Israel's desire is fixed upon Saul and his house. Despite Saul's protest that the Benjaminites are lowly among the tribes of Judah, Samuel wines and dines him and furnishes him a bed for the night on the roof. It is quite common in the Old Testament to find people objecting to their calling: we might think of the prophet Jeremiah, who claimed that he was too young (Jeremiah 1:6). Nearer in time to Saul, Gideon objects to his calling to deliver Israel from the Midianites, on the grounds of the weakness of his clan (Judges 6:15). Saul's statement about the Benjaminites is probably historically true, yet Hannah's speech in 1 Samuel 2:8 has paved the way for God to raise up the weak and lowly to positions of power.

The way Samuel wines and dines Saul in the presence of 30 guests, and with special food, hints at an anticipatory coronation meal, or it could have covenantal overtones, meals often being used to ratify such arrangements. It is in the first part of chapter 10 that we have the climax: the Lord's anointing of Saul, privately by Samuel, as ruler over Israel. The use of oil is a sign of coronation.

The passage ends with notice that a sacrifice will be offered at Gilgal and that Saul must wait for Samuel's arrival—possibly an editorial gloss that paves the way for the story in chapter 13.

2 Saul is proclaimed king

1 Samuel 10:17–27

The official proclamation of Saul's kingship consists of a speech by Samuel at Mizpah, in which he reiterates God's deeds on behalf of his people and makes it clear, again, that the demand for a king came from the Israelites and involves a rejection of their saving God. The tribes are asked to gather to cast the lots (to express the divine will) that will determine the kingship. Either this tradition is in conflict with that in chapter 9 or this is a pretence at casting lots when, in fact, the kingship has been decided in advance. There may be some overlapping of different sources within these few chapters. A similar lot-casting is found in Joshua 7:14–18, where the process of casting lots identifies a guilty individual.

When the lot falls on Saul, he is found to be hiding among the baggage—which, again, suggests his reluctance to fulfil the role of king (see also 10:16, where he doesn't say anything about the kingship to his uncle, on returning the donkeys). This is the point of no return: Samuel proclaims Saul as God's chosen one and the people proclaim him king. Because this is a new institution in Israel, the rights and duties of kings are written down—and it is interesting that, in Israel, kings are always kept in their place, rather than being regarded as demi-gods, as in surrounding cultures. This perhaps reflects the ambivalence that was always felt in Israel about kingship. We are told of some dissent among the people: while the warriors support Saul, there are murmurings from others who refuse to pay tribute to him. Again we see the tension in the way this passage is constructed, between anti-monarchic feeling (vv. 17–19, 27, probably from the hand of the Deuteronomists) and pro-monarchic sentiment in the rest of the passage.

3 Samuel's farewell speech

1 Samuel 12:1–18

Now that King Saul is in place, Samuel's role as leader comes to an end. In his witness to the actions of God in the past (vv. 8–11), we have another historical retrospect, telling of the iniquities of Israel and how

God at every stage sent leaders to get the nation out of trouble. This is a kind of declaration of innocence on behalf of the Lord, paralleling Samuel's declaration of his own innocence in verses 1–5. Once again, we find anti-monarchical statements here, indicating that although God was their king, that was not enough for the people of Israel. Consequently a king was found—a situation to which God was prepared to adapt. But moral obedience is the prime thing, and the conditional statement is this: if the people follow God, and if the king follows him, all will be well, but transgression will be punished hard. Samuel verifies the speech and his own authority by calling on God to make rain, which he duly does, and so the people fear both God and Samuel.

This passage is thought to be one of those historical retrospects added by the Deuteronomists—a speech put into the mouth of a great man on leaving the stage. The historical recitation is typical of the Deuteronomists' style, and the anti-monarchical sentiments that arise, again, probably represent their hindsight opinion in the light of later failures of kings, subsequent to Saul. Again it is reiterated that it was the people's decision to have a king, and not God's. The other Deuteronomic indicator is the conditionality of the covenant with the king and people—the 'ifs' and 'buts' of their moral obedience or otherwise. It is made clear that these conditions refer especially to the king, who, if he transgresses God's command, will be punished. This passage has been likened by scholars to the language of a covenantal treaty, and it paves the way for Saul's demise, which begins in chapter 13.

4 Saul's hasty sacrifice

1 Samuel 13:1–15

The chapter begins with an incomplete account of Saul's reign, from the Deuteronomic redactors, before moving into the narrative proper. Saul's first act is to choose an army, and we are introduced to his son, Jonathan, who has command of part of the army. Initial success is a cause for celebration: it is not clear whether that success was Jonathan's (v. 3) or Saul's (v. 4), although it is possible that Jonathan's victories would be naturally credited to Saul as king. Undeterred, however, the Philistines start to muster their forces again. This causes some consternation among the Israelites, some of whom hide, others of whom tremble.

In verse 8 the focus shifts away from the battle to Saul's offering of the sacrifice that Samuel had instructed him to make. Saul waits seven days until the time appointed but Samuel does not show up and people start to drift off. Saul, in an attempt to show some initiative and leadership, offers the burnt offering without Samuel. As soon as it is offered, Samuel, as the spokesman of God, appears and scolds him. Saul explains his worry that the Philistines might have struck without his having made the sacrifice to ask for God's favour, but the wrath of Samuel and of God come down upon Saul. Samuel reveals that, because of this disobedience, Saul has lost his chance of being the first in a lasting line of kings.

This is a harsh punishment for a seemingly small crime, revealing a certain incongruity in the account. We might put this down to the presence of differing sources; alternatively, it might be seen as deliberate, with irony being a feature of the tale. Either way, it arguably presents God as unreasonably strict to the letter of acceptable behaviour—and the event is an excuse to start the process of getting Saul out of the way to prepare for the reign of David and his line. Saul is told that God is seeking someone else, 'after his own heart', to be king (v. 14), and clearly David is the referent here. We don't hear Saul's reaction but it must have been one of astonishment. Saul nevertheless gets on with the job in hand and leads the people up to the army to continue with the task of defeating the Philistines.

5 Saul and Jonathan

1 Samuel 14:24–46

Saul's mistake about the sacrifice is not his last and the cycle of stories builds up into a picture of a man who is finding it hard to cope. The narrator introduces the story with the opinion that Saul acted rashly: his rash act is to commit his troops to an oath, cursing anyone who eats food before evening. Presumably the motivation is to keep the men focused on the task in hand—to rout the enemy—but, as a result, the men become faint. When a tempting honeycomb is discovered with honey dripping out, the troops dare not eat it, but Jonathan, Saul's son, has not heard the oath and eats some honey before being told about it. Jonathan supports the view of the narrator that the troops would have been better off having eaten. They are indeed so hungry that after defeating some Philistines, they slaughter animals and eat them straight away, with their blood. This transgresses the law against eating meat with the lifeblood in it, found in Genesis 9:4, Leviticus 17:11 and Deuteronomy 12:23.

While Saul is keen to press on and kill more Philistines overnight, on consulting God, through the priest, he receives no answer, suggesting that a sin has been committed. This, of course, is clearly Jonathan's sin of eating the honey. Again, lots are cast to discover the guilty party. This time, Urim and Thummim are used—a system of lots mentioned in Exodus 28:30 and Leviticus 8:8, and usually associated with priests, possibly the equivalent of our modern 'heads or tails'—and Jonathan's guilt is revealed. When Saul insists that Jonathan must die, the people pressurize Saul into sparing him and utter a counter-oath calling on the Lord's name. Once again, Saul gives in to popular demand and his authority is challenged so that he is made to look weak and unable to keep his own oath. This leads to withdrawal from battle for a while.

6 Saul rejected as king

1 Samuel 15:10–31

Despite Saul's military successes, Samuel is privy to God's word that he regrets making Saul king. Once again, strict adherence to commands seems to be the order of the day—and Saul has disobeyed the Lord's latest command by keeping back some of the spoils of battle. Samuel appears to be angry about God's decision. He finds Saul pleased with himself, having just defeated the Amalekites in battle, but is perturbed by the sheep and cattle that seem to be present, taken from the enemy. When Saul explains that they are sacrifices to God, Samuel's reaction is a negative one: once again, Saul has acted with the people on his own initiative and has not utterly destroyed the Amalekites as instructed (v. 18; see 15:3).

In verse 17 Samuel says an interesting thing to Saul: 'Though you are little in your own eyes...'. This indicates Saul's lack of confidence in his leadership abilities and his tendency, therefore, to pander to the people. In some ways, this is understandable, since Saul was the people's choice in the first place, in the face of some opposition to the idea of kingship. Once again, however, Saul has not obeyed the letter of the Lord's command: keeping the spoil is the point at issue. Saul objects that he has fulfilled the mission and that the people took the spoil to sacrifice to God, not for any personal profit, but Samuel's retort is that sacrifices are less important to God than obedience (v. 22). In another speech, he states again that Saul has been rejected as king. This leads Saul to see the error of his ways, and he admits that he has tended to listen to the people, and asks for pardon—but it is not as simple as that.

Samuel prepares to leave but Saul holds on to him and inadvertently tears the corner of Samuel's robe, which prefigures a later incident in which David tears Saul's robe. Samuel takes this as a sign that the kingdom is lost to Saul and his line, and that nothing will change God's mind. When Saul begs Samuel to turn back and worship the Lord with him, Samuel agrees, but it seems to change very little.

Guidelines

The story of Saul raises some complex issues of fate and flaw. Was Saul destined to fail, as indicated by a number of the passages we have read? Was it his fate? It seems that he barely had a chance to prove himself, and committed some quite small misdeeds, before God's wrath was conveyed to him by Samuel because of Saul's lack of obedience. To lose the throne over a reluctance to wait a few more hours to offer a sacrifice seems a huge incongruity. Or was Saul a flawed man whose tragedy was to fail? He was tall of stature and yet described as 'little in your own eyes'. He was impatient and impetuous. He pandered to the people who, he knew, put him on the throne in the first place. He had his weaknesses, and perhaps those were the issue. Or maybe it was a mixture of fate and flaw, a deadly combination that led to his failure. We are reminded perhaps of some of the great Shakespearean tragedies, in which fate and flaw combine to lead to the demise of a great man—Macbeth, for example. We might reflect on the role of predestined fate in our own lives versus our own decisions, choices, strengths and weaknesses.

The Samuel–Saul relationship is an interesting one. Saul seems to find it hard to break away from Samuel, yet Samuel is always in the background, not allowing Saul full independence. Samuel seems to have the ear of the Lord in a way that Saul never has. Samuel therefore becomes the mediator of news from God, so that God never deals with Saul directly. Perhaps Saul is over-reliant on his mentor and never really learns to stand on his own two feet. Yet his mentor holds on to his special relationship with the Lord, and Saul comes across as a naughty boy in relation to the older man. There may be lessons for us here about the question of how far we remain indebted to those who influence and train us when we are young, and how far we need to break away and pursue our own course in order to fulfil our own destinies.

2–8 March

David

1 David is chosen

1 Samuel 16

Samuel's fondness for Saul comes out in the statement that he was grieved over him (v. 1), but God tells him to move on. There is a new king to anoint! Samuel expresses some fear that Saul, on hearing of his new mission, will kill him: it would be treason to anoint a new king with one already in place. Yet God has a plan to involve Jesse and his sons in a legitimate sacrifice, with Samuel bringing his own heifer. Interestingly, the sacrifice is to take place in Bethlehem, home of Jesse's line as descended from Ruth (David's great-grandmother). The people of that city are frightened of Samuel: these great leaders clearly inspired awe, as their power was known by reputation.

As Samuel looks at seven of Jesse's fine, upstanding sons, thinking that one of them must surely be the one chosen by the Lord, he is taken in by the stature and appearance of Eliab, which suggests echoes of Saul's tall stature (10:23). But the Lord opts for the youngest, David. The choice of the youngest is a regular feature in the Old Testament: Jacob is chosen over Esau in Genesis 25:23, and Ephraim over Manasseh in Genesis 48:8–22.

At the point at which the spirit of the Lord descends upon David and withdraws from Saul, to be replaced by an evil spirit (vv. 13–14), Saul's character seems to change; as readers, we become less sympathetic towards him. In a sense, he is still a victim of fate, yet we see him becoming gradually more threatened and more desperate. Then there emerges a scene of great irony, in which Saul's servants suggest calling someone (described by them as one whom 'the Lord is with') who plays the lyre, to soothe him and calm his troubled spirit. The musician turns out to be none other than David! Of course, Saul has no knowledge of the previous anointing, and we are told that he grew to love David and made him his armour bearer. The soothing effect of David's lyre playing makes the evil spirit depart. Thus Saul is lulled into a false sense of security and the dramatic tension is increased so that we are poised for the denouement.

2 David and Goliath

1 Samuel 17:24–51

This is the famous story of David and Goliath, the champion Philistine from Gath. All were afraid of him but only David dares to challenge him. He uses the term 'uncircumcised' of Goliath (vv. 26, 36), which was true of all Philistines and was often used as a generic term for them. There is a promise of enrichment for the man who succeeds in defeating him—and marriage to one of the king's daughters. David is not meant to be there—he is supposed to be tending the sheep—so his brother Eliab is cross with him, but David answers him back. David's words eventually reach Saul and he opposes David's desire to pursue Goliath on the grounds of his youth. It seems from this passage that the two do not know each other, which makes us wonder about the different sources of the tradition that may have been amalgamated here.

David is confident in his abilities, however, claiming experience in having protected his lambs from roaming beasts, so Saul allows him to continue, ironically saying, 'May the Lord be with you': he doesn't know that the Lord has already chosen David to be king and that God's Spirit dwells within him. He gives David heavy armour, which David cannot wear, being unused to it. Instead he is armed with just a staff, five stones in a bag and a sling.

Goliath mocks David and threatens him with death. He also calls on his own gods—and we recall Dagon, who fell in subservience to the presence of the ark of the Lord (5:3). David calls upon his God and gives a return threat, citing the power of the Lord and calling for witness to him from 'all the ends of the earth'. It takes no more than one stone to strike the Philistine on the forehead and stun him so that he falls to the ground (with more echoes of Dagon's submission here). David is then able to kill Goliath with Goliath's own sword and cut off his head, which leads the other Philistines to flee.

3 David, Jonathan and Saul

1 Samuel 18:1–16

We learn in this chapter of a friendship between Jonathan and David, so deep that they are described as 'soul-mates'. Jonathan makes a covenant with David, a sign of which is his gift to David of his robe and armour. This gift seems to indicate a handover of role, as we are told that David was then successful in war and was set over the army by Saul (v. 5). It may also ironically signify Jonathan's renunciation of his claim to the throne—in fact, already renounced for him by God. It certainly gives David the support of a key figure, whose loyalty would more naturally rest with his father, Saul.

We then have a little interlude from the female side: one of the roles of women was in singing victory songs and rejoicing at military successes on the return of the men. Saul is angered by the suggestion in their song that David's successes have outstripped his own, and, in fact, this is the first sign of his growing suspicion of David. It is swiftly followed by an incident in which Saul tries to pin David to the wall with his spear—probably an assertion of his own power. Ironically, David eludes him, not once but twice, and Saul realizes at this point that David, not he, is now the one blessed with God's Spirit. He casts David out of his household and sends him off to war.

David's successes are unbounded: Saul has to admire the boy and yet he realizes that David's popularity among the people is gradually exceeding his own. There is tension here in the fact that Saul has loved David, yet is gradually recognizing the threat that he poses. There is also a problem with Jonathan, Saul's own son, who is also captivated by David more than any other. Scholars have suggested homosexual overtones in their relationship but the text is not explicit on that issue: it may be simply an example of male bonding and mutual admiration. David later remarks that Jonathan's love was better than any woman's (2 Samuel 1:26).

4 David and Michal

1 Samuel 18:20–30; 19:11–17

David eventually receives Saul's daughter Michal's hand in marriage. Of course, this was supposed to have happened after he killed Goliath (17:25), but it is presented here as if Saul plotted the alliance in order to trick David and make him vulnerable to the Philistine threat. We are told that Michal loved David before the decision was made that they should marry, which is a precursor to her eventually showing loyalty to David in preference to Saul. It is ironic that David was loved first by Saul himself, then by Saul's son Jonathan and now by his daughter Michal: there seems to be an endless fascination for this man!

Saul presents the idea of the marriage as if he is making a generous offer to David to become his son-in-law as a result of his successes and popularity. On David's humble acceptance, Saul asks only that he give him, as a present, one hundred Philistine foreskins. As we have already seen, the Philistines were known as the 'uncircumcised ones', so this seems an apt 'gift'. Being a poor man, David would presumably have been unable to pay the usual bride-price due for a princess (cf. Genesis 34:12), and Saul would have known this—hence his right to demand some other gift. This act David duly fulfils before the appointed hour (to Saul's surprise, no doubt), so Michal becomes his wife. This was not the outcome Saul had hoped for, of course, and he becomes frightened of David's obvious favour with the Lord. David simply goes from success to success and Saul recognizes that David has become his enemy.

In chapter 19 we discover Saul's resolve to kill David, as first Jonathan and then Michal try to save him from their father. In verse 12, Michal helps him to escape by letting him out of a window of his house: possibly, this took him outside the city wall. It is interesting that Michal has an idol handy to use as a decoy: this might indicate that household gods, as represented by idols, were still known at this time (compare Rachel's theft from her father in Genesis 31:19, 34–35). Michal's trick is also a good example of female ingenuity. Saul is hurt that his own daughter has deceived him but she makes her loyalties clear. She lies, saying that David threatened her with death if she would not help him escape.

5 David spares Saul

1 Samuel 24

We join Saul's hunt for David. Saul goes into a cave to relieve himself and he doesn't see David and his men sitting there. A twist of fate that he should choose that very cave! David is urged by his men to take the opportunity for vengeance upon Saul and so he cuts off a corner of his cloak, all without Saul realizing. This could well be symbolic of David's later wresting the kingship from Saul (compare Ahijah's tearing of his robe in 1 Kings 11:29–31). David immediately feels guilty about it on the grounds that Saul is still king and the Lord's anointed, and blames his men for egging him on. Saul leaves, oblivious that he had actually found David. Later, David takes the opportunity to confront Saul. He bows in obeisance and tries to reassure Saul that he means him no harm, demonstrating with the cloth from his robe that when he had the chance to kill Saul, he abstained. He calls him 'my father' and in turn Saul calls David 'my son' (vv. 11, 16). Although they are father-in-law and son-in-law, these designations may show the underlying affection that they once shared.

David swears that he will not harm Saul, citing a proverb (not one known from the book of Proverbs) that indicates that wicked deeds come only from wicked people. He makes it clear that Saul's quest to kill him is excessive: David, in abasement, likens himself to 'a dead dog' or 'a single flea' (v. 14) and prays that God will vindicate him against Saul. Saul is contrite and weeps. He is relieved to have been spared and now seems to accept the fact that David will be king after him. He asks David only to spare his offspring so that his name will be remembered. Remembrance as a result of continuing generations is an important theme in Hebrew thought (see Job 42:16). David agrees to Saul's request. There is a strong parallel of this chapter in chapter 26, which suggests a doublet in the tradition (that is, two accounts of the same event from different writers).

6 The end of Saul's line

1 Samuel 31

We return to Saul for the last chapter and the sad tale of his end. The Philistines eventually get the upper hand and kill all of Saul's sons. This is tragic as his descendants are now gone at the hands of the enemy, David's oath apart. Saul himself is badly wounded and asks his armour bearer to finish him off in order to avoid being killed by a hated Philistine—a final act of defiance against the enemy. But fear of his king prevents the armour bearer from obeying the request, so Saul decides to fall upon his own sword. This is a rare example of suicide in the Old Testament. The armour bearer falls on his sword beside him.

Once their leaders are all dead, the army flee and the Philistines are able to take control. We are told that the Philistines return to the battlefield the next day to take their booty—a common habit in war. When they find Saul, they cut off his head as a sign of their dominance (compare David cutting off the head of Goliath) and send out word of their success. It is interesting that the news is sent 'to the houses of their idols' (v. 9)—presumably their temples—indicating a defeat by their gods of the Lord. The temple of Astarte (a goddess known from Ugaritic and Canaanite sources) is mentioned as the place where Saul's armour is put, and his body is pinned up on a wall for all to see. Saul's own followers, however, steal the body back, along with the bodies of his sons, and give them a proper burial.

Such was Saul's end: he fell in battle, not as a hero but as a defeated man who took the only honourable way out by falling on his own sword. In 2 Samuel 1, a variant account of Saul's death is related to David, who duly mourned the death of this ill-fated king.

Guidelines

It is always hard to see others going from strength to strength while, for whatever reason, we ourselves are struggling. Even those of whom we are very fond (perhaps especially them), who succeed where we fail, can lead us to feel jealousy and even hatred at times. So it was with Saul and David: Saul had loved David once, and his whole family was attracted to him, such was his clear charisma. Yet David kept getting the better of Saul, kept on having success where he failed, on the battlefield and in domestic affairs. David even had power over Saul, as the only one who could soothe his troubled spirit with his lyre-playing. Ultimately, Saul's children chose David over their father, and Saul must have felt left out in the cold—hence his excessive pursuit of David, hoping to have revenge upon him. At the final confrontation, however, David is so good and kind to Saul that Saul dissolves in tears, such is the depth of his conflicting emotions of love and hate. It is often said that love and hate are closely related emotions in that they both demand of us fervour and strong emotions. It is clear that both Saul and David felt strong emotions when it came to their relationship.

David is the golden boy of these chapters: he is the unlikely shepherd boy chosen to be king. He is the Lord's choice and, as a result, he is the champion at everything he undertakes. The narrator is at pains to exonerate him from all blame in taking the throne from Saul: David is presented as the innocent, chosen by powers beyond him and, in that sense, simply a pawn in God's game. It is made clear that he never wishes to harm Saul, even when Saul becomes irrational and difficult. There is a lesson here for us about good, loyal treatment of our betters, even when we might perceive that we are slowly gaining the upper hand. For example, we continue to have respect for the elderly even when their demise is clearly approaching: they don't cease to be individuals demanding our respect.

FURTHER READING

Peter Ackroyd, *The First Book of Samuel*, Cambridge Bible Commentary, CUP, 1971.

Walter Brueggemann, *First and Second Samuel*, John Knox Press, 1990.

Robert Gordon, *I and II Samuel*, Paternoster Press/Zondervan, 1986.

The Bible and urban mission

The city is not only a highly significant feature of human history and contemporary life. It is also a major biblical theme with around 1,400 references to specific cities or to the city as a social, political, economic and spiritual entity from the early chapters of Genesis to the final chapters of Revelation. In fact, the biblical narrative has been described as a journey from a garden to a city, from Eden to new Jerusalem.

Our world is increasingly urban, with over 50 per cent of humanity now living in cities for the first time in history. In some parts of the world megacities are developing, with an infrastructure inadequate to cope with their exponential growth. In other areas city centres are emptying of residents but urban sprawl ensures urban culture is ever more influential. The city, as the focus of power and nexus of communication networks, has always dominated society and shaped its surroundings.

The early Church was largely an urban movement with missionaries moving from city to city and urban churches reaching out into the pagan countryside ('pagan' originally meant someone living in the countryside). But during the Middle Ages the church was more at home in the countryside and it has struggled to adjust to an industrializing and urbanizing society.

Today the church is strongest in the suburbs and the market towns, and weakest in the inner cities and urban housing estates. But the city is crucial if we are to incarnate the gospel of Jesus Christ in areas of greatest social and spiritual need.

The first week of notes explores different aspects of the Bible's story of the city. Despite its origins in rebellious self-sufficiency and its frequent implication in oppression and harmful activities, its future is glorious as God redeems and transforms it. Throughout the Bible God is found moving towards the city rather than away from it; even when the theme is judgment there are signs of hope and promises of redemption.

In the second week we explore diverse ways in which the people of God are invited to share God's love for the city and participate in God's persistent urban mission. This invitation has often gone unheeded as, over many years, Christians have moved away from the city into the suburbs or beyond. Rural imagery has dominated our liturgy and hymnody, and growth in spirituality is often associated with rural retreats.

But God is constantly reaching out and calling to the city, according to the prophets, even if the people of God, like Jonah, are often looking the other way.

Quotations are taken from the New International Version of the Bible, unless otherwise stated.

1 Cities of rebellion

Genesis 4:10–17; 11:1–9

Cain built a city, the first mention of cities in the Bible. Not content with an invisible mark of security, he built a visible stronghold. Refusing to accept his punishment and rejecting God's offer of security, his city was a potent symbol of self-sufficiency and independence. Built away from the presence of the Lord, the city was named after Cain's son; his family and future were bound up in the city he had built.

This is not a promising start. The city represents humanity's alternative to fellowship with God, an attempt to feel secure and significant. Conceived in sin and defiance, it is birthed away from God's presence as if to exclude him. It is a concrete expression of self-reliance, but a symbol also of alienation. Alienated from the ground, we create a new environment for ourselves; alienated from other human beings, we build walls around ourselves; alienated from God we create a little world to rule. The city is our kingdom, our pride and joy, our greatest achievement —and yet the place we are least secure and most alienated.

The most famous of early cities was Babel. In Genesis 11 we learn about the motivation behind its construction and we discover something of God's response to city-building. Do you notice the similarity to Cain's motives—to make a name and avoid being wanderers? The famous tower proclaimed: 'Who needs a god if we can build our way to heaven?'

The builders' enthusiasm is evident, but their work was doomed. God intervened and the very thing they feared came to pass. Their language was confused, their unity and security were shattered and they were dispersed. Why did God intervene? Maybe the builders' pride was offensive, or maybe this intervention was merciful, slowing down the speed of human achievement, limiting our capacity to harm ourselves and our environment.

Unfinished Babel is symbolic: no city has ever been completed. The city is always a goal rather than an achievement. It can never replace the lost presence of God, prevent wandering and insecurity, or satisfy human aspirations. Only the city of God can do this. But that lies much further down the road.

2 Cities of refuge

Joshua 20

The city may represent human self-sufficiency and the rejection of God's protection, but God does not reject the city. Instead, he uses it wherever possible for gracious and caring purposes. God, it seems, loves cities. Scattered through the Old Testament are many indications of this. God's love for Jerusalem is well known, but Damascus also is called 'the town in which I delight' (Jeremiah 49:25), and Jonah is rebuked for not sharing God's concern for Nineveh.

The ministry of the prophets demonstrates this. 'Listen,' cries Micah (6:9), 'the Lord is calling to the city.' Although often this call warned of judgment, God cared enough for the city to send it messengers. Several prophets received thrilling revelations of urban life as it could be under the rule of God. The city of God is the heart of the Old Testament vision of a restored land, an unwalled but secure city.

And God uses the city to bless humanity. Psalm 107 celebrates city life, contrasting it with life in the desert and hostile countryside. Cities are products of human creativity, skill and industry. They are warped and corrupted but retain vitality and potential for good. The Old Testament writers celebrate their beauty, architecture and culture. The order and security they provide are welcome. In spite of their rebellious origins, God adopts the cities and graciously uses them to rescue the needy.

Designating 'cities of refuge' in the promised land is a wonderful example of God's willingness to engage with the city. He not only deigns to use the city, he even uses it in a way that recalls and redeems its inauspicious origins. Cain built a city as a refuge. Now God is establishing refuges—but with the significant difference that they were not safe havens for murderers, but only for inadvertent killers. Cain himself would not have found refuge in them.

This is truly redemptive—making use of the city in a way that recalls the motivation behind it, but without endorsing its sinfulness. The city is not transformed beyond all recognition: its unrighteous features are removed, but all that is positive and life-giving about it is affirmed.

3 Cities of revulsion

Zephaniah 2:15—3:13

The prophets highlight many urban sins. Each city has its own story—the militarism of Nineveh, the sexual perversion and injustice of Sodom, the gross affluence of Tyre. But five urban sins especially revolt the prophets.

Oppression: The rich oppress the poor, the strong oppress the weak, and rulers oppress their subjects. Through violence, bribery, slander and extortion, oppressors dominate the cities. 'Woe to the city of oppressors, rebellious and defiled!', cries Zephaniah.

Idolatry: The countryside was also full of idols, but several prophets castigate urban idolatry. Jeremiah imagines people walking past ruined Jerusalem asking, 'Why has the Lord done such a thing to this great city?' Because the city 'worshipped and served other gods' (Jeremiah 22:8–9).

Bloodshed: Cities are places of violence where innocent blood is shed. Ezekiel says, 'Woe to the city of bloodshed' and declares that 'the blood she shed is in her midst: she poured it on the bare rock; she did not pour it on the ground, where the dust would cover it' (Ezekiel 24:6–7). Do we hear echoes of Abel's blood crying out from the ground against the first city-builder?

Sexual immorality: Sodom and Gomorrah are infamous but many cities were centres of vice. However, Sodom and other cities were condemned for both injustice and sexual immorality (see Ezekiel 16). Many Christians emphasize one or the other, but sexual purity and social justice are both vital for healthy cities.

Pride: The arrogance and stubbornness of the city hinder it from responding to God. Zephaniah critiques this perversion of civic pride: 'This is the carefree city that lived in safety. She said to herself, "I am, and there is none besides me"' (2:15). This is the language of divinity and overweening pride.

So do we despair of the city? We surely cannot assume our cities are healthier. Cities are still places where the poor and powerless are victimized, centres of sexual 'freedom' and exploitation, dominated by temples to Mammon, plagued by violence and yet proud of their self-sufficiency. The good news is that God has not turned away from the city. In fact, God is on a mission towards the city.

4 Cities of renown

Psalms 48 and 87

The centrepiece of God's urban redemption plan in the Old Testament was Jerusalem. God's response to the development of cities was not to retreat to the countryside but to establish his own holy city. Jerusalem, the city of God, was intended to be a radical alternative, a city set on a hill, to show what a city could be like. What Israel was to be at a national level (a light to the nations), Jerusalem was to be at an urban level, a model of justice, joy, peace and renown for other cities to emulate.

Israel had not been a city-building nation. Apart from the enforced construction of grain cities in Egypt, they had not started building their own cities until the time of Solomon. They had inherited their earlier cities from the Canaanites. God had in a remarkable way protected them from the lure of city-building. It was only when other things started going wrong, specifically when Solomon married many foreign wives and embraced their gods, that Israel copied the surrounding nations and developed their own city-building programme.

Jerusalem was not built by the Israelites. Indeed, it was one of the last cities in Canaan to be captured by Israel. Hardly a worthy history for a capital city! But perhaps that was the point. God chose for his holy city a place that had no history, a city that could give Israel no reason to take pride in their achievements. The crucial thing about this city was not its glorious history but its glorious destiny.

Several psalms speak of Jerusalem in glowing terms. In Psalm 48 this city is the joy of the whole earth, a place of true and lasting security, a city to take delight in and be proud of in a way that does not diminish the glory of God. Psalm 87 shows us people clamouring to be admitted as citizens of this joyful city of God, a place of fountains and celebration. Jerusalem was a concrete sign that God had not rejected the city, a working model of the New Jerusalem that was coming. The eventual fall of Jerusalem and the deportation of its citizens to Babylon is one of the great tragedies of the Old Testament.

5 Cities of remonstration

Matthew 11:1–6, 20–24

Jesus' ministry embraced many cities. We often associate his miracles with rural settings, but most of his miracles occurred in the cities, including Korazin, Bethsaida and Capernaum—signs of God's kingdom coming to the cities and demonstrations of God's love for them. Jesus embodies God's persistent mission to the city.

But the cities refused to repent and welcome him—not least Jerusalem, over which Jesus wept because it had forsaken its true calling and was facing judgment. Note that Jesus addressed cities, not just individuals, treating them as corporate entities capable of repentance. Individuals in the cities had responded to him but the cities had rejected him. So Jesus remonstrated with them, pronouncing a 'woe' on the cities, a solemn denunciation not used lightly in the Bible but normally aimed at those who rely on security other than God. Jesus agreed with the prophets that the city is under judgment.

Jesus then added to the Old Testament list of urban sins yet another sin—the failure to recognize God's Son. His miracles were signs that pointed to him but they had been ignored. Elsewhere (Matthew 12:41) Jesus compared his own generation with the city of Nineveh: that city had repented at Jonah's preaching but the first-century cities had rebuffed one who was greater than Jonah. Here he compared Korazin,

Bethsaida and Capernaum with Tyre, Sidon and Sodom, which would have repented if they had seen his miracles.

Jesus' comparison of ancient and contemporary cities warns us not to relegate what the Bible teaches about the city to ancient history. Our cities are characterized by the same sins and worse. Whatever improvements modern cities might claim, the biblical perspective is that cities tend towards greater wickedness and degeneracy—except where the kingdom of God breaks in.

But there is a word of hope hidden in this otherwise solemn passage: 'if the miracles that were performed in you had been performed in Sodom, it would have remained to this day.' Sodom could have been saved! There is hope for wicked cities when the power of God is manifested.

6 Cities of revelation

Revelation 18:1–10; 21:1–5

The Bible's final chapters are a 'tale of two cities'. Babylon the great is the ultimate manifestation of the city as the place of sin, rebellion and demonic activity. But New Jerusalem, the city of God, beautiful beyond description and full of God's glory, will replace it and last for ever.

Babylon exhibits the worst features of all the cities—Nineveh's aggression, Sodom's sexual sin, Tyre's affluence, Old Testament Babylon's occult practices. Babylon is a haunted city, an urban nightmare, ripe for judgment. But it is still a city like any other. Music and culture, weddings and celebrations continue to the end. Most people are unaware of its degenerate state. Babylon is our city—at the point of destruction. The first time 'Hallelujah' appears in the New Testament is when Babylon falls (19:1): the end of this city ushers in judgment and a new creation.

No attempt to analyse the breathtaking vision of the New Jerusalem will do it justice. God has taken something so debased and corrupted and transformed it into something so glorious. The story of the city is one of the most wonderful demonstrations of grace in the Bible. For New Jerusalem is recognizably a city, with walls, gates, foundations and at least one main street. For centuries we have tried to build a city that will meet our needs, but now the perfect city of God descends from heaven as a gift.

Our wandering is over. The city has finally been liberated from the spiritual forces that oppressed it and is now a true home for humanity, filled with the presence of God in a way not experienced since God walked with Adam in the garden in the cool of the day. New Jerusalem is a garden city, a beautiful harmony of urban and rural. We will not return to some rural paradise; we look forward to a city, but the tree of life and the water of life are there too.

It was with this urban vision that the early church infiltrated the cities of the Roman Empire. Realistic about the city's sins, refusing to be fully identified with it because of their heavenly citizenship, they were nevertheless deeply committed to reaching the cities with the gospel. They were known as people who had turned the world upside down—and it was in the cities, and among the poor in those cities, that this revolution began.

Guidelines

The Bible is neither anti-urban nor naive about the capacity of the city for evil. Cities can be alienating and dehumanizing; they can also be places of justice, community and creativity. Many Christians and churches are in the suburbs, semi-detached from the cities on which they depend for employment, entertainment and resources. Maybe a deeper understanding of the biblical story of the city will inspire us to a new level of engagement with our city.

As you pray:

- Celebrate the remarkable grace of God that takes a symbol of human rebellion and transforms it into the home of redeemed humanity.
- Ask for insight into the city where you live or work—signs of brokenness and bondage, and signs of God's presence in the city.
- Reflect on your response to the double vision in Revelation: what will it mean for you to live in the light of these alternative urban futures?
- If you do not live in a city, pray for urban churches and mission agencies, that they may be good news in the cities.

1 Prayer

Genesis 18:16–33

Abraham did not live in a city. He was a nomadic herdsman who lived in a tent. His only connection with a city was that his nephew, Lot, lived in Sodom. But he did have an urban vision: he was looking forward to the city of God (Hebrews 11:10).

A message from angelic visitors that Sodom and Gomorrah faced judgment spurred Abraham to pray. Abraham had personal reasons for wanting the city spared, but Lot and his family are not named in his prayer. Abraham's prayer is for the city, pleading that it will not be destroyed if there are a handful of righteous citizens there.

His prayer has been called a 'prayer of negotiation'. From fifty down to ten Abraham reduces the number needed. There he stops and goes home satisfied God has heard his prayer and will act justly. Abraham has fulfilled his responsibility, and God promises to show mercy if there were just ten righteous people in the city. In fact, the cities were not spared. But Abraham's prayer was answered in the rescue of Lot and his family. The angels told Lot they could not destroy Sodom until he left, so firmly was God committed to his promise to Abraham.

What will stir us today to pray for the city? Perhaps, like Abraham, one particular city will provoke our compassion, a city where we have connections or about which God speaks to us. Nehemiah was stirred to pray for Jerusalem by a report from his relatives (Nehemiah 1:1–4). Daniel was moved by what he read in scripture to pray, 'Give ear, O God, and hear; open your eyes and see the desolation of the city that bears your Name' (Daniel 9:18). For Jesus, the sight of Jerusalem in the distance caused him to weep over it (Luke 19:41).

Abraham's prayer for Sodom can be a model for us as we pray for our cities. We are to remind God that there are righteous people in the city; we can pray that God will spare the city for the sake of what is good in it; we can plead that the innocent are not swept away in indiscriminate judgment. Cities can be spared—if they have righteous inhabitants and the people of God pray for mercy.

2 Presence

Jeremiah 29:1–7

The exiles were confused and homesick. The unthinkable had happened; Jerusalem had fallen and they had been deported to Babylon. Why had God allowed his city to be destroyed? Was God still with them in this alien city?

Jeremiah's advice was clear: God has placed you in Babylon; don't expect to escape in the near future; settle down and make your home in the city; get involved in its life and activities; raise families and build community there; get rid of negative attitudes and seek the city's good.

What relevance does this have to contemporary urban mission? Few Christians are in the city as war captives; most have the option of moving out. But it is as true now as when Jeremiah wrote, and when Abraham prayed, that the presence of God's people in the city can make a difference. Prayer for the city can be offered from a distance, but many answers depend on us getting personally involved.

The church in the city has been weakened by the small number of Christians moving into the city and the large number moving out. Suburban churches are growing at the expense of inner-city churches. Two strategic changes are needed if we are to share in God's urban mission: many Christians living in the city need to stay there, and many Christians elsewhere need to move in.

It was not enough for the exiles to live in Babylon. Jeremiah urges them to get fully involved in its economic and social life; to raise families there and to plan for future generations still living in the city. They were also to pray for the city—not against it—aware that their destiny was caught up with Babylon's. Their goal was the shalom of the city.

Shalom is a rich concept that requires commitment to the total well-being of the community. Seeking shalom in the city means a caring ministry towards the many hurting, lonely, marginalized people who live there. It means working for structural changes that will increase peace and justice in the city. And it means praying for its prosperity—a just distribution of opportunities and resources for the good of all.

3 Prophecy

Jonah 3

Why was Jonah reluctant to go to Nineveh? Prophesying to this hostile imperial city was enough to make anyone quail, and his message was uncompromising. But he was also afraid the city would be spared. Jonah agreed with God that Nineveh was wicked, but he did not want it saved. God loves the city but many of us have written it off—ready to condemn its wickedness and not convinced it is worth sparing.

Jonah's message is blunt and totally negative. Was this God's word to Nineveh? We know God longed to have mercy on the city, but Jonah speaks only of destruction. Indeed, we imagine him rubbing his hands together in anticipation! This is not false prophecy, for Jonah's message is accurate, but he has not communicated God's heart towards the city. He has expressed God's anger about the city's sin but has omitted God's desire to spare it.

Despite Jonah's bad attitude, despite his inadequate message, Nineveh repented and was spared. The overwhelming response is unparalleled in the Old Testament. God's grace is such that the brusque message of this grumpy prophet produced a city-wide response.

The response began among ordinary people. The king's decree was important in that it represented the official reaction of the city authorities, but it was largely redundant: the citizens were already doing what was decreed. The anticipated outcome—Jonah's imprisonment or execution and suppression of popular discontent—never happened. Revival came to Nineveh.

What does it mean to prophesy to the city? What is it about our city that concerns God? Jonah addresses the city as a whole but speaks only about 'wickedness'; Nahum later condemns Nineveh for violence, arrogant militarism and economic oppression. What might God put his finger on in our city?

The church in the city is called to be a sign, a prophetic community. The day of the isolated prophet is over: ever since the incarnation made the word flesh, the prophetic ministry has needed a community to speak out from, a community with a shape, ethos and lifestyle that gives integrity to the message of its prophets. The building of such communities, fully part of their localities yet radically distinct, is a primary task of urban mission.

4 Preparation

Nehemiah 2:11–20

If any biblical book can be described as a manual for urban ministry, it is the diary of Nehemiah. Jerusalem lay in ruins. Many years had passed since Nebuchadnezzar had devastated it; some of the exiles had returned and there was an attempt at community life. But life was tough, resources were scarce and an air of despondency hung over the city.

Far away in imperial Susa, a report reached Nehemiah: 'Those who survived the exile and are back in the province are in great trouble and disgrace. The wall of Jerusalem is broken down, and its gates have been burned with fire' (Nehemiah 1:3).

For four months Nehemiah fasted and prayed for the city before receiving permission to go to Jerusalem. Three days after his arrival he began to prepare for the task ahead. He thoroughly inspected the walls to see what needed to be done and was left with no illusions about the size of the challenge. He encountered opposition. Sanballat and his friends were offended by his arrival, accused him of empire-building and ridiculed his hopes. Finally, knowing he could accomplish little alone, he assessed the workforce. He had a list in his mind of who would do the work—even priests and nobles would be asked to work—but he said nothing yet. The success of his mission depended on willing volunteers who caught his vision for a city rebuilt.

There are lessons here for anyone contemplating urban mission. Don't rush in with preconceived ideas; don't alienate local people or take them for granted; don't be surprised by opposition. Humility, discernment and patient preparation are needed. In urban communities trust needs to be won and hopes rekindled: they may have lived with ruined walls for a long time. And we must count the cost of urban mission: the city is a centre of opposition to the purposes of God. Time spent listening, looking and learning will not be wasted.

When we have done this, we may be ready to declare to the powers that dominate the city: 'you have no share in Jerusalem or any claim or historic right to it' (v. 20). The powers have usurped the city, but they have no right to it. In the name of Christ we have come to rebuild and restore.

5 Power

Acts 19

The city, in the Bible and throughout human history, represents power. Cities are the places where powerful people live, influential movements operate and conflicts occur between those wanting to exercise power over others. So urban mission often involves power encounters, as the kingdom of God clashes with the powers at work in the city—political, ideological, religious and economic.

Ephesus had many competing religions and philosophies: the Jewish synagogue, a Greek debating hall, occult practitioners, self-styled exorcists, the cult of Artemis, as well as disciples of Jesus. Spiritual power (good and evil) was close to the surface: sorcery, demons, healings, exorcisms as well as tongues, prophecy, and 'extraordinary miracles'. Economic interests were entwined with religious practices and politicians had to engage with both.

Western commentators since the Enlightenment have struggled with passages like this, but our cities are increasingly hotbeds of interconnected spiritual, economic, social and political power struggles. In our cities, as in Ephesus, competing interests will vie for attention, and mission must be flexible and holistic.

Here we have half-converted disciples with defective theology needing to receive the Holy Spirit and be baptized in Jesus' name; three months evangelizing in the Jewish community, provoking mixed reactions and public hostility; a change of strategy and change of venue; two years of public debate with both Jews and Greeks; extraordinary miracles, power-imbued handkerchiefs, healing and exorcisms; a self-appointed Jewish priest and his exorcist sons using Jesus and Paul as magic names and finding that this attempt to manipulate spiritual forces caused problems; a massive bonfire of expensive occult textbooks prompted by fear of the Lord whom Paul proclaimed; and a riot and anti-Christian demonstration.

What a mixture of planned and unplanned mission; of careful long-term work and sudden explosions of activity; of arguing persuasively and simply watching God at work; of scepticism, fear, joy, conviction, opposition, imitation and the unexpected!

And what a wonderfully understated conclusion: 'in this way the word of the Lord spread widely and grew in power' (v. 20)! Urban mission is messy, exciting and often conflicted. Are we daunted by the challenges or excited by the opportunities?

6 Patience

Revelation 3:7–13

Urban mission will not be accomplished overnight. It will not be achieved by hit-and-run projects, by ministers 'doing a stint' in the inner city before graduating to more prosperous and congenial locations, or by initiatives that spring up suddenly and die equally quickly, like the plant which sheltered Jonah as he waited for God to zap Nineveh (Jonah 4:5–7).

Writing to seven city churches, John calls himself 'your brother and companion in the suffering and kingdom and patient endurance that are ours in Jesus' (Revelation 1:9). He invites them to embrace all three realities. Urban mission is tough and requires patient endurance. God's kingdom has broken in through the death and resurrection of Jesus, but other kingdoms are resisting this. The powers, including the power behind the city, have been conquered and disarmed, but they are still at large. Our task is to point towards what God's tomorrow will be like. Doing this in the cities is vital, because of what the city represents: the rejection of God's plans, and humanity's attempt to build its own tomorrow.

Patient endurance is one of the main themes of Revelation. The phrase 'him who overcomes' which is repeated many times can be translated 'him who endures to the end'. Victory in the New Testament is not triumphalism. It is the ability to stand firm patiently.

There is work to be done; there are opportunities for service. In Philadelphia the city church is shown a wide open door: the church may feel weak and weary, as many urban churches do, but the day of opportunity is still present. The reward for faithful service is a share in the coming city of God. If we want a share in that city, we have work to do in ours.

Revelation begins with a vision of Jesus and ends with a vision of the New Jerusalem. The city of God is still future, a hope which inspires urban mission and enables us to endure, but Jesus is already enthroned and at work. In him the kingdom has already arrived. City churches, like all others, are living in the in-between time, testifying to the kingdom of God and praying for its consummation.

Guidelines

The cities of our urbanizing world now represent the primary mission frontier for the church. If we do not discover how to incarnate the gospel in the cities, no amount of church growth in the market towns, suburbs and villages will prevent the church from becoming a marginal influence in contemporary society.

It is in the cities especially that Christians are encountering the challenges of injustice and poverty, ethnic tension and relations with other faith communities, and evidence of the end of Christendom and the influence of secularism and post-modernity.

The call to urban mission is for all followers of Jesus who look forward to the coming of the city of God. Some may need to stay in the city rather than moving out; others may need to move in and seek shalom in the city. Some may pray for God's mercy on the city nearest to them and for God's kingdom to come in power and grace.

Ponder quietly the challenge of the urban mission context.

- What is God calling you to do?
- What will it cost you to respond?
- What resources will you need?
- Who can you talk to about this?
- Where will you start, and when?

FURTHER READING

Jacques Ellul, *The Meaning of the City* (Eerdmans, 1970): a classic text on the city in Scripture, tracing the story from Genesis to Revelation, full of insights but pessimistic about the potential of the city.

Bob Linthicum, *City of God, City of Satan—A Biblical Theology of the Urban Church* (Zondervan, 1991): another survey of biblical teaching on the city, which brings out clearly the double-edged nature of urban culture and the city's potential for good or evil.

Stuart Murray, *The Challenge of the City* (Sovereign World, 1993): another survey of the city from Genesis to Revelation, more hopeful than Ellul, highlighting biblical insights on urban mission.

Ray Bakke, *A Theology as Big as the City* (IVP, 1997): a presentation by a leading urban missiologist of major biblical themes relating to the practice of urban ministry.

Mark Gornick, *To Live in Peace: Biblical Faith and the Changing Inner City* (Eerdmans, 2002): rooted in personal experience and redolent with theological and biblical reflection, a rich resource for contemporary holistic urban ministry.

Michael Eastman & Steve Latham (eds.), *Urban Church: A Practitioner's Resource Book* (SPCK, 2004): with contributions from many urban practitioners and multiple short chapters, a very accessible introduction to the practicalities of urban mission and urban church life.

Laurie Green, *Urban Ministry and the Kingdom of God* (SPCK, 2003): reflections on the changing urban mission scene, drawing on decades of experience in the inner city, illustrating key theological themes.

www.urbanexpression.org.uk: the website of Urban Expression, an urban mission agency inviting Christians to get involved in mission in the cities of Britain.

Zechariah for Today

In some respects Zechariah is the most difficult of all the minor prophets despite the fact that we know perhaps more about the background and date of this book than we do for any of the others. Like them it calls for imagination, but whereas the other minor prophets describe life as they see it and invite us to enter imaginatively into it, Zechariah stimulates our imagination by his use of visions, symbols and images. We therefore always need to be alert to the dangers of finding in his book whatever we want. To minimize this, take trouble to get into the background. See if Zechariah's situation rings any bells for you, whether it be in your own country, local community, church, club or elsewhere.

Up to a century earlier, in the extremely tough circumstances of exile in Babylon, the élite had managed to survive and on the whole seemed to have done well for themselves, whilst the poorest people had been forced to seek a living there. By the time we get to Zechariah, the exiles, some of whom had made good in Babylon, were beginning to return. Some were shocked at the conditions back home where traditional beliefs and expressions of religion were at a low ebb. Others had developed a more modern, cosmopolitan outlook which was shocking and disturbing to those who had never been away. Some found the arrival of the returnees, not to mention the 'foreigners' who were now also coming in, unacceptable, especially when they threw their weight about. Zechariah finds himself living in a divided community. Each needed the other. Each resented the other. Differences of approach, experience, situation and culture made life difficult. What was needed was someone with a vision. That man was Zechariah.

Unlike some of the prophets who seemed weighed down with the situation, Zechariah has a message of hope. A new day is dawning. Joy is round the corner, and it is neither the result of a political turnaround nor the fruit of human effort. It is utterly and entirely a victory for God.

Don't worry too much about what Zechariah is trying to say to his generation. Try rather to identify with the overall situation. Read the text with at least one eye (even both eyes) on your own situation and hear what Zechariah is saying, not to them then but to us now. If you find that difficult (and you may well), don't give up. Let it wash over you and soak into your skin. The chances are that at certain times, sooner or later (and maybe sooner than you think), you will find a refreshing drink in a thirsty land.

Be aware that when you move from chapter 8 to chapter 9 you may feel as if you are in a different world. Scholars have noted this and some have suggested a different author and a different date, possibly about 200 years later. More recently, however, the trend has been to try to see it as a whole, which is how the compilers of the canon saw it and how it has come down to us.

Unless otherwise stated, all quotations are taken from the New Revised Standard Version of the Bible.

1 A new world

Zechariah 1:1–17

These people had been having a hard time for longer than most of them could remember, though many of them grew up with stories of a past that was either idolized or idealized, or both. Self-esteem was low. Hopes were meagre. Those who had never had anything had little to look forward to. Those who had, failed to find it satisfying. Life went on, in many respects, almost unchanged and unchanging, but there was not much heart in it for anyone. Each successive generation produced its theories and reasons, but running through them all was a common thread. The Almighty was much displeased or (to put it differently) they were on the wrong tack. Then suddenly there was to be a time of peace (v. 11)

Europe went through a similar experience at the time of the Reformation and immediately afterwards. Many, if not all, Europeans experienced something similar in the 20th century and especially in the 1990s. The experience is universal, whether you find it in empires, nations, churches, organizations, families or individuals. The cry is always the same: where did we go wrong? How can we make amends? What do we do to ensure we get it right next time (v. 12)? Zechariah has no direct answers but can offer a few hints to point us in the right direction.

First, the prophet does not deny the past, but he gives us a slightly different version of it. The Babylonians and Persians all had a part to play in the purposes of God. But Zechariah sees these nations, which were used by God to punish Israel, as having taken the punishment further than God really intended. This has led God to be angry with the pagan nations and even more positive in his return to Israel. This viewpoint emphasizes the hand of God in all of Israel's experiences, positive or negative.

Second, we can recognize that what is right in one situation does not necessarily have to stand for all time. Not everyone will find it easy to accept Zechariah's attribution of a change of heart and mind on the part of the deity (vv. 15–16), but it should not be difficult to appreciate that circumstances change things, our perceptions of God change, and he may reveal himself in different ways in different times and situations.

2 A global world

Zechariah 2:1–5

The new 'Jerusalem' is to be of a size never previously contemplated, with a recognition of the animal world alongside people—what today might be described as 'global' with a modest green emphasis. But the idea may not appeal to everyone in the same way.

What do you feel, for example, when you see a man outside your house with theodolite, tapes and a ruler? Joy? Thank goodness someone is taking action. Plans are being drawn up. A new development must be on the horizon. Or fear—even suspicion? 'Young man, what are you doing with that?' Of course we need action. We have been saying so for years. But who is up to what? And when and where? Questions flood the brain and may be more an indication of our basic attitudes than of any serious intent to acquire information. So what do you think were Zechariah's first thoughts when he saw someone in the city with a measuring rod?

How then do you read his emotions when he hears they are planning a town without walls? A brilliant idea, you might think. Openness and freedom. A world in which everyone can come and go. No more passports, visas and planning control. A huge oyster waiting to be cracked open and no more big defence budgets.

But wait! Freedom to go out means freedom for others to come in. People may have forgotten that their ancestors were immigrants—a rabble of slaves who bulldozed their way into Canaan—but the thought of anyone being able to walk into a city without walls is enough to strike apprehension if not terror into the most placid of individuals. Who will come? What will they be like? What will they do? And (most important) what will it mean for us?

For people with such conflicting emotions and interests Zechariah offers encouragement. God is a caring God. The size of the city and the population is something God can handle. Defences will not be needed because he will care for it. It will be a new expression of his glory (v. 5). Could he mean that when we widen our horizons, welcoming other people and even embracing other cultures, we may discover a fullness of life not previously contemplated? Whatever the answer, it certainly seems to call for patience and a long haul. The Jews were still wrestling with the Gentiles in the time of Paul.

3 Law and order

Zechariah 5:1–4

The bigger a community grows, and the more varied its members, the more complex its rules, regulations, traditions and unwritten codes of behaviour become. Children first experience this when they go to play with friends and find a whole new list of dos and don'ts. Tourists find it in foreign countries; receiving communities find it when tourists arrive. Business and commerce experience it with foreign contracts and immigrant labour.

In the case of Zechariah, some scholars have suggested that the tensions of living together might have arisen partly as a result of those who had stayed behind in Palestine refusing to relinquish land to those returning from Babylon. That may or may not have been the case, but overall Zechariah's appeal to all sides is to show respect and concern for others and integrity in all their dealings.

The flying scroll may reflect this. Its length (almost 30 feet) is not unusual. Its breadth (15 feet) is phenomenal. Most scrolls were no more than a foot wide. If we assume that its content has to do with behaviour (right and wrong) then its size suggests an enormity and a variety of offences. Ten commandments and two clay tablets may have been sufficient for the earlier, more simple and homogeneous community. The emergent new community, with established residents, returnees and first-time immigrants made any discussion of law and order a far from simple affair. Think of the difficulties of law and order in a community which has undergone similar changes, say, in medieval times, or the Reformation, or even your own childhood.

So what are we to make of the 'flying' scroll? Perhaps it suggests a world of uncertainty, variation, fluctuation, a world subject to wind and weather—very different from anything like the tablets of stone or 'the law of the Medes and Persians which altereth not'. Imagine the feelings of those who had seen little change in 1000 years but for whom the whole world now seemed to be collapsing around them.

This is hardly a word of hope or encouragement. It's more like the head teacher saying what they will/will not tolerate. But if the image helps us to appreciate our own situation, it might also help us to begin to think how we could handle it and what message we may take to heart and pass on to others.

4 Ambassadors for God

Zechariah 6:1–8

This is not an easy vision to interpret, and the explanation given by the angel does not help much. If we accept the idea that Zechariah's vision needs to be seen against the fact that the Mesopotamian sun-god was depicted as rising between two mountains, we may assume that Zechariah saw the four chariots as messengers (or ambassadors) from God with a job to do in the four corners of the earth. The black horses are despatched to the north country, the white to the west, and so on.

What they are to do is unclear, but verse 8 seems to suggest that success is establishing some kind of stability which would 'set at rest the spirit' of the Almighty. In other words, if Yahweh is pleased because things have settled down a bit in the north (Babylon), this is what he (and presumably Zechariah) would like to see happening everywhere else. So it might be worth asking what could have brought about the change in the north. There are several possible answers.

The most likely is 'a new boy on the block' in the person of Darius, ruler of Persia, with a more open attitude to religious beliefs. He seems tolerant of faiths other than his own, willing to lift some of the restrictions under which immigrants and minorities have been living, and, far from exploiting them, is more than ready to give those who wish to return the right to return and those who wish to stay the right to stay. Of course, the ambassadors to the south and the west are going to find things different, but if the essence of their role is to set at rest the spirit of the Almighty their overriding task is no different. Peace, harmony and freedom for people in general (and for the Jews in particular) is what matters.

Ponder Zechariah's vision in the light of your own experience. What would such ambassadors for peace need to address in your situation? What is needed, in the place where you are, to bring 'rest to God', and what can you do as ambassadors to bring it about?

5 Ambassadors of experience

Zechariah 6:9–15

At this point the story line becomes a little clearer with Zechariah's call for recognition to be given to those who have returned from Babylon and for an open policy allowing others from afar to make their own contribution to the building of the temple (vv. 10, 15). There is some uncertainty over the names and responsibilities but the overall sense seems to focus not so much on the transference of power (from the residents to the returnees) but on the recognition of the wider experience which not only the returnees but all who come from far away have to contribute. 'Excellent,' you might say. But why is it excellent? And what do you think were Zechariah's motives? There are several ways of reading these verses.

One possibility is that it was all a matter of power and authority. Zechariah was afraid the newcomers would take over and build the temple their way. This is not in the Bible text, but it may well have been in the background because he is careful to clarify that the ultimate authority will stay where it was, in that despite the honour being given to Joshua and the returnees (vv. 11–13) he has already made Zerubbabel ultimately responsible for the rebuilding from start to finish (4:9). Is Zechariah trying to appease those who share his worries, and take advantage of the new experience of the returnees whilst at the same time retaining control?

A second possibility is a charitable, if slightly grudging, attitude to the stranger within the gates, as if to say, 'We don't really want these people but now they are here we must treat them with respect. Better to have them working with us than against us.'

A third option is that Zechariah is offering an open-handed welcome to the possibility that the returnees and their friends can not only supply knowledge and experience but also help to handle (even solve) previously difficult and convoluted situations, and thus bring an entirely new stimulus to the enterprise that is lacking in zeal or flagging with familiarity.

Never mind Zechariah's motives. What, in your situation, should you be doing? What are your heart and mind telling you to do? Finding satisfactory answers will put you on the first step towards understanding what it means to welcome Ambassadors of Experience.

6 Not fasting but righteousness

Zechariah 7

What happens when a community fails to hear what God is saying to them? With social change and a more cosmopolitan community, people find themselves asking (and being asked) all sorts of questions they never thought of asking, or preferred not to think about, as long-standing customs and unquestioned traditions come under the microscope. Some people seem able to survive happily without honouring practices which have always been regarded as essential to a faithful life. Some feel under threat. Some genuinely want to consider what matters and what doesn't.

In this case it was a matter of religious ceremonial, regarding fasting and abstinence from strong drink (v. 3). A minor question perhaps to some, like whether I need to close my eyes when I pray or whether I need to say my prayers every day, but not minor to the people who are asking it. Think of many similar examples from your own experience.

Zechariah's first response is to suggest that the people examine their motives. In all the years they insisted on doing 'whatever it was', why did they do it and why was it so important? Was it really for God, or was it (like eating and drinking) something they did for their survival and personal satisfaction? Was it to give them a feeling of security? Did they feel something terrible would happen if they didn't? And what did they think it could do for God? It is a very searching question, calling for an honest answer from Christian people in every generation.

To help them to find the answer, Zechariah suggests that they listen to what the prophets were always telling them in their perceived 'golden age' or the days of prosperity. What most concerned the prophets was how people lived their life. Commitment to basic human rights and the way they behaved towards their fellow humans must come before arguments about the minutiae of religious belief or practice (vv. 9–10).

Then comes the sting in the tale. The people didn't listen then and they are not listening now. Yet it was because they failed to heed what was said, and not only failed but in some cases resolutely set themselves against it (v. 11), that they found themselves in the troubles they had just been going through (v. 14).

Guidelines

- Identify some of the problems of living in a global world, with fewer barriers and instant communication, more tourism and immigration, and different cultures living more closely to each other. Think about it in the light of what Zechariah says in 2:1–5 and, if you have the opportunity, raise the issues in a local discussion group.
- Looking at the people within your immediate group or environment, try making a list of the rules and customs which cause most friction. What suggestions could you make to improve relationships?

- Exercise your imagination on the four horses (6:1–8). Start with the idea that where there is trouble we may have to intervene (like the black horses, setting God's spirit at rest) and where there is not we have a responsibility to prevent it arising (perhaps like the other horses). Which situation do we find ourselves in?
- In the light of 7:1–14 make a list of religious rituals in your own life and another of similar but different rituals among your friends. How do they compare and what happens when you talk to your friends about them?

1 City of truth

Zechariah 8:1–17

This is Zechariah on a good day, with a clear mind and words of inspiration and encouragement. Hope oozes in the pauses. Things are going to get better. Read quickly through these verses and get an overall picture of the new Jerusalem as Zechariah sees it. Don't stop to ask whether it ever turned out like that and don't spoil it by suggesting that perhaps he was being over-optimistic. Notice rather what he sees and highlights as the marks of a godly community and consider whether you and he are looking in the same direction when *you* think of a godly community.

After portraying the world of his dreams (vv. 4–8, 12) and comparing it with how things used to be (vv. 10–11), verses 16–17 sum it up. A godly community is marked by respect for truth, justice and peace, and genuine respect for one another.

Now re-read the passage more slowly and consider how much your dream of the future chimes in with Zechariah's, and what would be needed to achieve his ideal in your situation. For Zechariah the basic essentials are three.

Firstly, truth. A city where people are open and honest with one another, of course. But try to work out what more is needed for a city to be called a 'city of truth'. Is it something to do with structures as well as people and attitudes? If it is, what does it say about structures? If not, what is it?

Secondly, a city where there is room for all: old people and children, plants and animals (vv. 4–5, 12), and where other people want to come and live and work (vv. 7–8).

Thirdly, no shortage of jobs, and adequate rewards (v. 10).

Now stop your dream, wake up and plan action. One act might be to give thanks for those places where you can find some or all of those features in your immediate community. Another might be to identify those places where they are absent, or present but defective, and think what you can do about it. A third, if you wish to go deeper, might be to give some thought as to how local structures might need to change before your 'city' could ever be described as 'a city of truth', and where you would need to begin.

2 Festivals and tourism

Zechariah 8:18–23

Imagine a people for whom religion has been a burden, not perhaps in the sense that they found it unattractive, boring or too demanding, but in the sense that it always left them with a feeling of inadequacy. Whatever they did, they could never quite hit the mark. What appeared to work for others just didn't quite work for them. Religious ceremonies and occasions were not so much solemn as serious—extremely demanding in every way but unimaginative and unsatisfying. Confessions and long faces were always more in evidence than thanksgivings, celebrations, fun and laughter. None of it was necessarily a reflection of God, but it was certainly a reflection of human perceptions of God in their society, and it always made worse when the prophets were out like wasps.

Then comes along Zechariah with a new vision. At least four of the fasts are to have an element of gladness at the centre. The origin and purpose of the fourth, the seventh and the tenth are not known and some scholars have even suggested the fifth may have been an addition, but why not allow for a little hyperbole: 'the fifth is going to be an occasion of joy—and every other feast you can imagine as well.' Zechariah has the bit between his teeth. He wants to change the mood and give the people an uplift.

As Zechariah waxes eloquent, so the picture changes from a city for which nobody cared to one which everybody wants to visit. A neglected tourist spot suddenly becomes top of the list for holiday brochures. A 'sink housing estate' suddenly spawns a new image and the price of real estate rockets. The downtown church with a dull notice board and a leaking roof, patronized only by three old people and a dog, suddenly boasts a congregation that blocks the entrance and lifts the roof. Its people too become more desirable. The day was when nobody wanted to know them. Now people queue up to claim their acquaintance.

But consider the consequences. What is the effect on the faith (and the faithful) when everybody is included and its very popularity puts it in danger of becoming something it was never intended to be? What then is the role for a new prophet?

3 A new policy

Zechariah 9:9–17

After a few minor changes we come to a whole new way of life: lordship replaced by humility, war by peace, and the mighty horse by a donkey.

According to Matthew 21:5, whatever verse 9 meant to Zechariah and his contemporaries, when the friends and disciples of Jesus saw him riding into Jerusalem on a donkey this was the verse and the image they called to mind, even if according to John 12:16 his disciples did not really know what to make of it until much later. What might have attracted them to this verse? Was it that they recognized a different idea of kingship? Was it his persistent refusal to take up arms? Or was it simply the extremity of the symbolism? And how come they only understood it after the resurrection? Perhaps it was only when the clouds cleared and the sense of what they had been witnessing over the last three years dawned upon them that they re-read Zechariah and suddenly made the connection.

For Zechariah and the Jews it was different. The cold war, for them, was over. For a thousand years they and their forebears had been having running battles with the superpowers Egypt, Persia and Babylon. Now

Zechariah and his friends begin to sense the dawn of a new day when life was going to be different. As with Jesus 500 years later, the mould of traditional thinking had been broken. Zechariah sensed people warming to the idea of accepting others as they were rather than as they wished they were, as he wrestled with the reality of getting all the new inhabitants of Jerusalem to relate to one another instead of quarrelling, bickering and scoring points. Maybe the disciples began to see in Jesus something not entirely new but something similar to what Zechariah had in mind.

Five hundred years later the dream was still not fulfilled. It still isn't, but this doesn't stop Zechariah from dreaming about it, nor Jesus from expressing it, nor the disciples from proclaiming it. It may indeed never be attained in this life, but that is no reason for not rejoicing, because it is dreams like this that every so often cause that flash of lightning after which life is never the same again. Those are the moments that change us and, in changing us, change the world around us.

4 A new democracy

Zechariah 10:1–4

A new world, a new policy, a donkey instead of a warhorse, and a more caring and peace-loving God, all suggest the time has come for a different kind of leadership.

Inevitably, this gets through to the people before it is recognized by the leaders, who in any case always want to hang on to power. Their day is doomed. Trusted sources of information (intelligence) and power (advice) have failed to deliver. The teraphim (or household gods, v. 2) represent ancient traditional religion no longer relevant in a modern age. Those who claim to know what is going to happen based on an analysis of past experience (diviners) and those who seek to inspire the people with plans, programmes and theories (dreamers and visionaries) are only too often misreading or distorting the facts and raising false hopes. Spin and salesmanship did not arrive at the end of the 20th century, and we may be left to guess who Zechariah might have in mind were he with us today.

A different kind of leadership is not the same thing as a different set of leaders. It might mean a recognition of leaders who have been there all the time but were overlooked because our idea of leadership goes back to a different kind of God. Zechariah's understanding of God is not so much powerful, male-dominated and macho, but more of a good shepherd. He will still have his cohorts but his cohorts are going to be the sheep (the people) who must no longer see themselves as sheep (i.e. followers). They are to become a trusty horse. They are to take the power and the responsibility into their hands. They are to be the source of God's power, not simply recipients of what their leaders offer. They are also to be the warriors, but warriors of a different kind with a different set of objectives and therefore a different range of enemies.

So what will they do? Mainly, hold things together, like the corner-stone that holds two walls together (v. 4), stick to their task with the firmness of a tent peg, and fight to build something new rather than creating havoc and lining their pockets.

Once you have identified the people in your community who are desperate for the spring rains (vv. 1–2), where do you find the sort of people Zechariah has in mind in verses 3–4, and what qualities are you looking for?

5 People power

Zechariah 11:4–14

People power may emerge as a rebellion against established leadership but people power also usually has to have its own leader. Zechariah sees that as his role. Try to put yourself in Zechariah's position.

Reflect on the different 'worlds' which have come to mind in your own experience over the last ten days as you have been trying to enter into the community in which Zechariah found himself. Choose one, preferably small, local and manageable, where you sensed even the vaguest possibility of people power asserting itself. You are Zechariah. What might you say or do?

Your heart bleeds for the way in which your family, friends or colleagues have been victims of bad leadership (false shepherds). Instead of complaining you hear the call to assume the role of shepherd. No point in becoming one of the ruling shepherds. That would be joining the club to influence the club, like getting on to a committee to take part in what the committee is manifestly failing to do. What people power requires is not just a different leader but 'something different', and it begins with one person (or a small group) operating in a totally different way. See if Zechariah helps you to think it through.

First he makes a break with past and present leadership. See his staff (Favour) as an image of caring, and breaking it as an expression of what he feels about the shepherds and their caring methods. Apparently they have no doubt what message he is sending out (v. 11). So what alternative has he to offer?

Secondly, he has the courage openly to accept that some things need to die and some things need positively to be destroyed. Since he does not specify exactly what he has in mind you can fill in the details from your own experience.

Thirdly, unlike the leaders he is rejecting, who are little better than hirelings, he is prepared to accept personal and total responsibility for those most needing his care and protection.

Fourthly, having fractured his first staff to mark a break with the past he now introduces his new staff, Unity. What he has done others must do, and he must rely on his own personal example and commitment to give them the inspiration they need. They are to be shepherds to one another. This is what will hold the flock together.

Here is the 'something different' that was so badly needed.

6 New Jerusalem

Zechariah 12:1–9

Here we see a picture of the triumph of Jerusalem over all the surrounding people. It is not clear what Zechariah means by 'Jerusalem'. He may be thinking of Jerusalem as a city or as a symbol of everything that Jerusalem stood for in the context in which he was working, much as we might refer to Hollywood or Moscow. Think of it therefore as a collective noun for the triumph of those values which Yahweh, the Jews, Zechariah and his colleagues represented and stood for in the light of their history, where they had come from and what they had always striven for.

The specific values they treasured may not resonate easily with the world we live in. Christianity long ago added a dimension Zechariah could never have contemplated, and in the last 50 years in Europe the exclusivity of the Judeo-Christian tradition and the hitherto unquestioned Western values developed in the years of Reformation and Enlightenment no longer have universal acclaim. It might be better therefore to begin where we are and to focus our hope on those ultimate values which today we regard as crucial. What are they? Where do we find them and how can we establish them? When we do, we may notice that some of their roots lie deep in those earlier traditions of which Zechariah and his contemporaries were aware.

For example, coming to terms with the totality of creation and the place of humanity within it (v. 1). Surrounding forces (that is, other nations) may well lay siege to the values (that is, Jerusalem) but can never conquer them or destroy them. Those who try to destroy them will only finish up destroying themselves like people getting hernias from trying to lift something beyond their strength (v. 3). The enemy will panic and go mad and the people (if not the chiefs) will come to see the superiority of what we stand for (vv. 4–5). At the same time we may have to recognize that Jerusalem (the values) cannot succeed in isolation. Support may be needed from quarters previously ignored or rejected if we are to achieve our objectives, and the day will come when we, like Jerusalem, have to come to terms with the fact that we will never supersede those other forces which will continue to have their own identity (vv. 6–7).

Guidelines

- Determine five values you would expect to find in a godly community or ask five of your friends to suggest one each. Compare them with Zechariah's list. How many can you recognize in your community? What would be needed to make up what is missing, and what would be needed before your community could claim the accolade of being a 'city of truth'?
- Imagine a situation where new people have taken over and changed everything so much that what you grew up on and meant so much to you is barely recognizable. Now imagine a prophet speaking into that situation. Try writing a script for him.

FURTHER READING

R.J. Coggins, *Haggai, Zechariah, Malachi*, Old Testament Guides, Sheffield Academic Press, 1996.

Paul L. Redditt, *Haggai, Zechariah, Malachi*, New Century Bible Commentary, Marshall Pickering, 1995.

Brevard S. Childs, *Introduction to the Old Testament as Scripture*, pp. 472–87, Fortress Press, 1979.

Charles M. Laymon (ed.), *The Interpreter's One-Volume Commentary on the Bible*, Abingdon Press, 1971.

DYING TO LIVE

Passiontide: the days are longer but the darkness deep. In the season of temptation in the wilderness, there must have come a day when the hunger pangs were greatest and the devices of the devil the hardest to resist. On the journey to Jerusalem, there must have been a point when the desire to turn back was excruciatingly difficult to suppress. Jesus did not want this way, and yet he chose it. As the darkness deepens, so we are confronted with the theme of suffering and death. It is not an easy theme and there will be some questions from which we would rather shy away.

The poet Stevie Smith surprised by saying 'I love death, I think it's the most exciting thing. As one gets older one gets into this—well it's like a race, before you get to the waterfall, when you feel the water slowly getting quicker and quicker, and you can't get out, and all you want to do is get to the waterfall and over the edge. How exciting it is!' We may question whether we can, or should, ever share such a sentiment entirely. Death is the very antithesis of life and is never something to trivialize or underestimate. And yet, because of Jesus, death has lost its sting, its poison, its power to hold. In these days leading up to Easter, we will look at what it means to die daily to self in order to live eternally in Christ. We are going acknowledge our mortality in order to look forward to our immortality. These may be painful studies, but we undertake them with our gaze fixed on Christ—the suffering servant who leads us into life.

As a guide, we take both the words of scripture and the scripturally inspired words of some of the great hymn writers. During the first week of readings, we ask where we hear of death and dying in Jesus' pre-Passiontide earthly ministry, and what these references have to say to us. During the Holy Week readings, we try to get a sense of Jesus' attitude towards his own suffering and death. For our 'Guidelines' sections, we look to the writings of another poet, Emily Dickinson. When Dickinson put pen to paper in the mid-19th century, her writing was so startlingly different and mould-breaking that she was considered unpublishable. When the first volumes of her poetry did finally get into print, their content was described as 'poetry torn up by the roots'. During the coming days, we too are invited to tear up at the roots our inhibitions about death and dying and to ask the difficult questions, that we may walk with greater abandon in the way of the cross.

These notes use the New Revised Standard Version of the Bible.

1 Dead and buried

John 12:20–36

Lead, kindly light,
amid th'encircling gloom,
lead thou me on;
the night is dark,
and I am far from home;
lead thou me on.
Keep thou my feet;
I do not ask to see
the distant scene;
one step enough for me.

From 'Lead, kindly light', John Henry Newman (1801–90)

When Newman wrote these words, he was stranded in Italy. He later described how he was 'aching to get home yet for want of a vessel was kept at Palermo for three weeks'. So there was a literal reality underlying the lines that have encouraged many people over nearly 200 intervening years. This hymn was sung as a solo on the *Titanic* the night before it sank. It was sung by Betsie ten Boom on her way to the concentration camp at Ravensbruck, from where she did not return but travelled on into glory. 'Keep thou my feet... one step enough for me.'

John 12:24 is often quoted to encourage self-denial, but reading it again in its original context we may gain a new appreciation of just how momentous a statement it is. The Son of Man uses the image of a grain of wheat to refer to the Son of Man. In the teaching of Islam, Jesus, or

Isa, does not die on the cross but is 'raised alive unto God'. In the teaching of Jesus, we learn that if he had not died, the Son of Man would have been about as significant as a grain of wheat. He foretells that because he dies (vv. 31–32), the ruler of this world will be driven out, and he, Jesus, will draw all people to himself. Bumper harvest!

'But if it dies, it bears much fruit' (v. 24). These words are primarily about Jesus but also refer to our attitude to life. If we are to learn their lesson, we need first to recognize the vulnerability of the one who voiced them: 'Now my soul is troubled' (v. 27). Letting go is never easy, especially when you hold the world in your hands. Jesus knew that the path he was travelling was going to get darker. In many ways, Newman's hymn is an echo of Jesus' guidance in verses 34–36. We need to search our own hearts. Can we learn the contentment of which this hymn speaks? It may get dark, very dark, but carrying the Christ-light within us we need not look very far ahead. The only way to progress on this journey is to take it one step at a time.

2 Carpenter's son

Luke 2:41–52

Time, like an ever-rolling stream,
will bear us all away;
we fade and vanish, as a dream
dies at the op'ning day.
From 'O God, our help in ages past', Isaac Watts (1674–1748)

'O God, our help in ages past' is a paraphrase of Psalm 90, a psalm that deals with the difficult topic of the length of our life. Nevertheless, neither the psalm nor the hymn has a despondent or hopeless feel: they name our weakness and fragility and the fleeting nature of our earthly lives, but place them in context alongside God's compassion, glory, and steadfast love.

The Bible passage for today is the story of how Joseph and Mary spent three agonizing days searching for the boy Jesus, not realizing that he had stayed behind in the temple after the festival of Passover. This is the last time we hear of Joseph in the Gospels. Although Jesus is later referred to as the son of Joseph (Luke 4:22; John 1:45; 6:42) and the 'carpenter's son' (Matthew 13:55), Joseph himself makes no further appearance. At the beginning of Jesus' ministry, it would seem that Mary attends the Cana wedding feast without him (John 2:1). She is mentioned along with Jesus' brothers on several occasions (Matthew 12:46; Mark 3:31; Luke 8:19), but Joseph is not named. Mary is there at the cross, and Jesus asks the beloved disciple to look after her (John 19:26–27).

'Time, like an ever-rolling stream, will bear us all away.' The convention in works of art has been to depict Joseph as an older man. It is quite likely that he died when Jesus was still young, and that Jesus experienced at an early age what it was to grieve the death of someone close to him. This is another reminder that Jesus 'stood where we stand' and 'walked where we walk'. He had to come to terms with his own mortality and with that of those around him. 'Cast all your anxiety on him, because he cares for you' (1 Peter 5:7). The glimpses we get of Jesus' close relationship with his heavenly Father suggest that the child's cries for help had developed into a life-sustaining habit of private prayer.

3 Oaths and dinner guests

Mark 6:14–29

Inspired by love and anger,
disturbed by endless pain,
aware of God's own bias,
we ask him once again:
'How long must some folk suffer?
How long can few folk mind?
How long dare vain self-int'rest
turn prayer and pity blind?'

FROM 'INSPIRED BY LOVE AND ANGER', JOHN L. BELL AND GRAHAM MAULE

We are not told how or when Joseph died, but we do learn of the manner of John the Baptist's death, and it is shocking. John died as the result of a double evil—the cruel manipulation of Herodias and the cowardice of

Herod the king. A certainty in all of our lives is that we will one day die, but we are justified in flinging questions like stones at God's door when we hear of a horrific or untimely death.

John Bell and Graham Maule are contemporary hymn writers, full of passion for justice and compassion for the hurt of the world. Their writing spits out the interrogation that others are unable or hesitant to utter. We know that God's bias is to the poor, the suffering, the underdog, so how can he allow the apparent proliferation of injustice in the world?

Another strange omission in the Gospels is that we are told nothing of Jesus' reaction to the death of his cousin John. We add to the mounting list of questions: 'Where was Jesus when John needed him?' and 'Surely he could have intervened?' Matthew's version of this appalling story recalls how John's disciples 'came and took the body and buried it; then they went and told Jesus' (14:12). So Jesus could not intervene because he did not know: he is fully human and once again he is confronted by death. His reaction is to withdraw in a boat to a deserted place (Matthew 14:13). We are not even told that he went apart to pray. Did he seek out the barren place *because* of his own emptiness, his gaping pain and grief? In days to come, how would he channel these feelings, and was it his own reaction of love and anger that would keep him on course for the cross?

Are there 'why' questions that you need to put to God? Whether for the first or the 50th time, it is important to keep on asking. It may be that as you stay with the questions, you also sense that God is calling you, equipped by grief, to respond in love and anger to the needs of a hurting world.

4 Dismiss your servant?

Luke 2:22–40

Frail children of dust,
and feeble as frail,
in thee do we trust,
nor find thee to fail;

thy mercies how tender,
how firm to the end!
Our maker, defender,
redeemer, and friend.

FROM 'O WORSHIP THE KING', ROBERT GRANT (1779–1838)

The words of the Nunc Dimittis have given comfort and assurance to countless generations of Christians. They express trust in God, a sense of peace and completeness, and the knowledge of salvation. What always amazes me, though, is Simeon's parting shot. He did not 'go gentle' into the night: 'This child is destined for the falling and the rising of many in Israel, and to be a sign that will be opposed so that the inner thoughts of many will be revealed—and a sword will pierce your own soul too' (vv. 34–35). Why did Simeon feel the need to say words like this, to declare an agony that Mary would experience all too soon? What kind of blessing is this?

I wonder whether Simeon's words might be a necessary expression of frailty. There are still societies today in which older people are esteemed, honoured and sought out for the wisdom of their years, but they are few and far between. Older people are disregarded because we consider it shameful to slow down, acknowledge weakness or cherish the past. This sensibility is, of course, all about externals. The reality before God is that all of us are 'feeble as frail', and the hymn writer Robert Grant was deeply aware of it. Born in India in 1779, the son of the East India Company's director Charles Grant, he spent his life working for those who were struggling or socially disadvantaged. In 1834 he became governor of Bombay, a post that he held for only four years, dying in July 1838. The local people grew to love him and the second oldest medical college in India is named in his honour.

Simeon's blessing speaks of the one whose very presence will unveil our true selves. This unveiling is painful and costly but Mary, by her obedience, has already accepted that no price is too high to pay. The staggering reality is that it is the real me, the real you, and not the external appearance we aspire to, that is made in the image of God (see 2 Corinthians 3:18). How do you feel about the process of ageing? For most of us, it is something we struggle with. How can we learn to see this process as the opportunity for the revelation of Christ in us, the hope of glory?

5 Not dead

Mark 5:35–43

Word of mercy, giving
succour to the living.
Word of life, supplying
comfort to the dying.
FROM 'LORD, THY WORD ABIDETH', HENRY WILLIAMS BAKER (1821–77)

Baker's hymn expresses the sufficiency of the Word made flesh. It speaks of the experience (or the conviction) that Christ, the living Word, comes to us and meets our need, whatever our current circumstance. Jairus, on approaching Jesus, gave repeated expression of his need: 'My little daughter is at the point of death. Come and lay your hands on her, so that she may be made well, and live' (5:23). He asked not for comfort for the dying. He asked nothing less than life restored.

Delayed by the woman with the haemorrhage, Jesus is yet to set off when messengers come and tell him that the little girl has died. There is much that is strange and wonderful about this incident, and we may wonder why Jesus feels it necessary to stress that the child has not died. Is this a healing miracle or a resurrection miracle, and does the distinction matter? Perhaps what is going on here is Jesus' gentle nudge to turn from self-absorption to selfless love. The hollow self-interest of the mourners is highlighted by their ability to switch from mass hysteria to mockery in seconds. Jesus' comments about commotion would seem to question the authenticity of their grief, but his words of comfort and assurance to Jairus are very different. Jairus, in his demand, has demonstrated a remarkable gift of faith and so Jesus warns him of the danger of distraction, saying, 'Do not fear, only believe' (v. 36).

How does reading a passage like this help us to handle our own grief? Surely it is salt in the wound to say that Jesus raised the dead when we cannot expect our own loved one to rise from the coffin and live? We need to remember that all of the Gospel miracles pointed to one thing: who Jesus was and is. They authenticated his power and his presence. Sometimes we do see similar miracles today, but standing as we do on this side of Easter, on this side of death and resurrection, we recognize that a little girl alive, the Nain miracle and all the rest were road signs to a destination. Their immediate impact on families was companionship for a few more years, but they pointed to a reality which is life in its fullness, always.

6 Dozing?

John 11:1–44

In suffering be thy love my peace,
in weakness be thy love my power;
and when the storms of life shall cease,
Jesus, in that tremendous hour,
in death as life be thou my guide,
and save me, who for me hast died.
FROM 'STILL NIGH ME, O MY SAVIOUR, STAND', CHARLES WESLEY (1707–88)

What do tears say? When loved ones are hurting, and when we share their hurt, we long to be with them. Yet for God's glory and for the sake of the disciples, Jesus chose to be apart. John highlights the almost unbearable tension that Jesus must have felt when he stresses that although he loved Martha and her sister and Lazarus, 'he stayed two days longer in the place where he was' (v. 6). When Jesus does at last make the journey, and when he meets with the two sisters in turn, each has identical words to say: 'Lord if you had been here, my brother would not have died' (vv. 21, 32)—words that cut to the heart.

As in the story of Jairus' daughter, Jesus speaks in terms of sleep, not death. But this seems to confuse the disciples, and he goes on to make it quite clear that his words are euphemism, intended to soften the blow: 'Lazarus is dead. For your sake I am glad I was not there, so that you may believe' (v. 15). The scale of the Lazarus miracle is something altogether new. Not only is Lazarus dead but, by the time Jesus does arrive, he has been dead for four days. It is an extremely costly miracle for Jesus, requiring him to postpone a journey he longed to make at once.

The story of Lazarus is one that speaks eloquently of separation—not only the agony experienced by the sisters but the agony of Jesus himself. It speaks volumes of their love for him but also of his love for them and for Lazarus. Jesus, fully man and fully God, lived out a love that was about intimacy, not abstraction. He lived out a love that needed others, a love that said to Martha, Mary, Lazarus, 'I long to be with you and I cherish all that makes you who you are.'

A brief, painful separation was necessary to fulfil God's purposes. A little later, the violent separation of the cross would be a difficult and inevitable separation, achieving the continuous presence which is the promise of Charles Wesley's hymn. Think about the times when you have felt Jesus close at hand and the times when you have felt him to be distant. Use this verse of the hymn to help you confront fears of loneliness or abandonment. Claim the promise of Jesus to be with you always, even to the very end of the age (Matthew 28:20).

Guidelines

A toad can die of light!
Death is the common right
  Of toads and men—
Of earl and midge
The privilege.
  Why swagger then?
The gnat's supremacy
Is large as thine.

FROM *SELECTED POEMS*, EMILY DICKINSON (1830–86)

Dickinson's pithy observations are a wake-up call to reality and a lesson in humility. In the course of this week's readings, we have considered some of Jesus' encounters with death and dying during his earthly ministry. At the most basic level, they remind us how he, like any other human being, had times of subjection to loss and grief. Look back over these readings. What can we learn about Jesus' reactions, and which questions remain unaddressed? Is there a sense in which Jesus' experience of death shaped his own response to God's call? Perhaps you have suffered recent bereavement or you are walking alongside others who are struggling with loss. How might Jesus' behaviour inform your own, and how does his understanding speak into your situation or that of those you seek to support?

1 Buried at baptism

Romans 6:1–4

O generous love! that he, who smote
in Man for man the foe,
the double agony in Man
for man should undergo.

FROM 'PRAISE TO THE HOLIEST', JOHN HENRY NEWMAN (1801–90)

In his final prison letter before his execution at the hands of the Nazis in 1945, Dietrich Bonhoeffer wrote the following: 'This is the end, for me the beginning of life.' For Christians, there is a double sense in which death becomes a beginning. As Paul writes, baptism is a kind of burial. Our old self is buried with Christ by baptism into death, so that, 'just as Christ was raised from the dead by the glory of the Father, so we too might walk in newness of life' (v. 4). And then there is the physical death that Bonhoeffer describes. It may look momentous, final and terrifying from one perspective, but from the perspective of eternity it is a way in and not a way out.

As we begin the second week of Passiontide, we are aware that Jesus has now entered into Jerusalem, the hollow 'Hallelujahs' of Palm Sunday have been sounded, and the steps remaining to the cross are not too many to count. These are days when Jesus' own earthly existence will flash before him—the loss of loved ones, the lessons learnt and taught, the family and friends from whom he has taken leave. These are lonely days, days when he has to put one foot in front of the other, come what may. These are self-emptying days, days of obedience 'to the point of death—even death on a cross' (Philippians 2:8).

As we reflect on the final stages of the journey, we revisit the hymnody of John Henry Newman. The double agony was an agony *in* Man *for* man. That God's own Son could live a human life and die an excruciating and ignominious human death is the scandal of Christianity, but it is a scandal that leads us to fall on our knees in adoration and gratitude. 'O generous love!' says Newman. This is generosity on a scale that we can scarcely even begin to comprehend. It is God's letting go of God: 'Unless a grain of wheat falls into the ground and dies...'

This week is Holy Week. It is an opportunity and invitation not to 'get a grip' but to lose it, to surrender our control and, in humility, respond to God's call. How can you loosen your grip this week? What will it mean for you to put one foot in front of the other for God?

2 Out of poverty, everything

Mark 12:41–44

Were the whole realm of nature mine,
that were an offering far too small;
love so amazing, so divine,
demands my soul, my life, my all.
FROM 'WHEN I SURVEY THE WONDROUS CROSS', ISAAC WATTS (1674–1748)

In the midst of the hurly-burly of these last days, Jesus sits down opposite the treasury to indulge in a little people-watching. In all the drama and tension of the moment, he makes space for a poor widow and two small copper coins. He meditates upon her gift. This offering would seem too small but, out of her poverty, it is everything. As we too ponder this scene, this apparently insignificant action, we are reminded of a different poverty—the poverty of a back yard in Bethlehem. Remember the Irishman who was asked by a stranger how to get to a certain place: 'To get to there? Well, I wouldn't start from here.' Impossible journey? Who would have thought that the journey begun at Bethlehem would culminate at Calvary, or that its object would be the salvation of the world?

Isaac Watts was born on 17 July 1674 in Southampton. The eldest of nine children, he was the son of an educated deacon in a dissenting Congregationalist church. The family knew the meaning of suffering: at the time of Isaac's birth, his father was in prison for his non-conformist beliefs. Isaac began to write when he was very young, and today's hymn has been called the greatest in the English language. Much of the time, he based his verses on the Psalms, but he also wrote controversial compositions known as 'hymns of personal composure', based entirely on personal feelings. 'When I survey' is one such hymn.

It is impossible to estimate how many people have been inspired by singing these lines. They succeed in expressing our highest desire—to give all that we are in response to the one who has given all for us. As Watts says, the love which is so amazing demands everything. But the question is, will we give it? It is more than likely that you will sing these words on a number of occasions this week. Would you be able to write a sequel verse, telling what it has looked like for you to respond freely to love's demand?

3 Be prepared

Mark 14:1–9

Heav'n shall not wait
for triumphant hallelujahs,
when earth has passed
and we reach another shore:
Jesus is Lord
in our present imperfection;
his pow'r and love
are for now and then for evermore.

FROM 'HEAV'N SHALL NOT WAIT', JOHN L. BELL AND GRAHAM MAULE

The theme of these studies is 'Dying to live'. We must take care that we adopt neither of two equally dangerous attitudes. The first is that we make death a taboo and, in so doing, deny the reality of who we are. The second is that we become so obsessed with death and dying that we forget to live life in the here and now. Today's readings present a corrective to this second attitude.

Just two days before the Passover, an unnamed woman creates a spectacular scene. There's a certain similarity with yesterday's widow, for this too is a woman with treasure. This woman is of ampler means, however, for the value of her nard is measured in denarii (v. 5) and not mere copper coins. Who knows how long she had saved to secure her gift? A gift squandered, or that's how the do-gooders feel. Had *they* sold their goods already and passed the profits to their neighbours in need?

Judas Iscariot was one who raised an objection to what had taken place. John, in a parallel passage, includes as an aside a remark about Judas' disregard for the destitute and dishonesty in keeping the common purse (John 12:6). The woman's extravagance and Jesus' reaction seem for him to have been the final straw. Judas ups and leaves and goes to the chief priests. They promise him a booty, not a donation for the poor.

This is at once a painful and a beautiful story: painful because of the reactions of the onlookers, especially Judas, and beautiful because of the woman's action and Jesus' promise: 'Wherever the good news is proclaimed in the whole world, what she has done will be told in remembrance of her' (v. 9). What are we to make of Jesus' comment that the woman anointed his body for burial? From our standpoint this side of the cross, these words do not sound quite as shocking as they must have been for listeners way back then. The woman's behaviour was criticized by the onlookers as foolish extravagance. Is there a sense in which we are delaying our devotion to Jesus? Heav'n *shall* not wait. Jesus is Lord in the here and now.

4 Kingdom coming

Mark 14:24–42

By thine hour of dire despair;
by thine agony of prayer;
by the Cross, the nail, the thorn,
piercing spear, and torturing scorn;

by the gloom that veiled the skies
o'er the dreadful Sacrifice;
listen to our humble cry,
hear our solemn litany.
FROM 'O SAVIOUR, WHEN IN DUST TO THEE', ROBERT GRANT (1779–1838)

At this stage in Holy Week, we are entering the darkness before the dawn. Jesus bends language as he declares, 'I will never again drink of the fruit of the vine until that day...' (v. 25). Although he can speak of future glory, he must now enter a darkness where the light of the kingdom cannot shine, a darkness so dark that it seems it will never end.

In accordance with Jewish tradition, Jesus and the disciples end the meal by singing the 'Hallel', or praise psalms. As they go out to the Mount of Olives, Jesus tells them something they cannot bear to hear: 'You will all become deserters' (v. 27). Although he points to the picture of a scattered flock in Zechariah 13:7, the disciples do not believe him. It is possible to feel alone in company, and this is certainly a moment of complete isolation for Jesus. 'I am deeply grieved, even to death; remain here, and keep awake' (v. 34). C.S. Lewis once described the impact of his own grief as like 'an invisible blanket between the world and me'. Jesus and his disciples have spent years in one another's company, but on this darkest night, this 'hour of dire despair', the disciples seem oblivious to the emotional turmoil of their master.

The hymn 'O Saviour, when in dust to thee' is not one we sing frequently these days—for obvious reasons, perhaps. However, if there is a time for this hymn, it is when we recall the darkness of Gethsemane immediately before Jesus' arrest. The verses list the different trials that he endured, some not quite so self-evident as others. The expression of pain and suffering, of self-denial and self-emptying in this hymn is almost entirely unrelenting, and it is only in the very last lines of the last verse that we find an affirmation of death defeated and hope restored.

There are times in our lives when we need to acknowledge the darkness, when it is impossible to 'look on the bright side' or 'sing a happy song'. Christians are not always very good at recognizing this. Paul's injunction to 'Rejoice in the Lord always' (Philippians 4:4) is not about a superficial merriness to be conjured up on demand. It is about the recognition that no matter where we are, and no matter how we feel, the Lord is near and he reaches out to us in love.

5 Forsaken

Luke 23:33–49

Thy comeliness and vigour
is withered up and gone,
and in thy wasted figure
I see death drawing on.
O agony and dying!
O love to sinners free!
Jesu, all grace supplying,
turn thou thy face on me.

From 'O Haupt voll Blut und Wunden', P. Gerhardt (1607–76), tr. Henry Williams Baker (1821–77)

This ancient hymn is based on a 14th-century Latin poem which meditates on Christ's body as he hangs on the cross. There are a number of different English translations, but this one follows Paul Gerhardt's German version. It is usually sung to a melody by Hans Leo Hassler, written around 1600 for a secular love song. J.S. Bach arranged this melody and used it five times in his *St Matthew Passion*.

Luke's account of the crucifixion contains careful detail about the reactions of those who were witnesses to what took place at Golgotha. There were the soldiers, who gambled and scoffed. There were the two criminals, one who mocked and one who repented. There was the centurion who looked on and declared Christ's innocence. There were the crowds who turned out for a spectacle and went home beating their breasts. And finally, and surprisingly, there were '*all* his acquaintances, including the women who had followed him' (v. 49)—his mother Mary included, of course: 'a sword will pierce your own soul too' (Luke 2:35).

Where do we see ourselves among the bystanders at the cross? Today's hymn is written in the first person. Who is speaking? The repentant thief? The centurion or one of the women? Or is it me? As we read these lines and ponder the horror of what took place, we are also reminded of the depiction of the suffering servant in Isaiah: 'He had no form or majesty that we should look at him, nothing in his appearance that we should desire him' (Isaiah 53:2). The face of death is such that we wish only to turn away. Yet, paradoxically, the lines of the hymn quoted above end with the entreaty that the dying one turn to us. Is this an entreaty that you will carry in your heart today?

6 Won!

1 Corinthians 15:50–58

Love's redeeming work is done;
fought the fight, the battle won:
lo, our Sun's eclipse is o'er,
lo, he sets in blood no more.

FROM 'LOVE'S REDEEMING WORK IS DONE', CHARLES WESLEY (1707–88)

'Two into one doesn't go.' There are some feats that, no matter how hard we try, we cannot achieve. In today's passage from 1 Corinthians, Paul stresses that flesh and blood cannot enter the kingdom of God. In order to enter into eternal life, we will need to let go of our earthly body. There are no two ways about it. But this is not a condemnation or a threat; it is a transformation.

During his lifetime, Charles Wesley wrote over 7000 hymns. The four short lines quoted above are a tiny fragment of this vast stock of creativity, but they are four lines packed with imagery and wisdom, and are worth spending time with. Love's redeeming work is God's redeeming work, and so we are reminded that God *is* love—no more, no less. We often speak of God as loving *and* powerful, or loving *and* faithful, or any number of other combinations of qualities. When we truly understand that *God is love*, we will also appreciate how all the rest must follow.

The battle language of the hymn echoes the saying that Paul quotes: 'Death has been swallowed up in victory' (v. 54). Nowadays, this kind of language is unpopular and there are hymns that we quite rightly decline to sing because of their stridently militaristic overtones. But to speak of a fight here is vitally important. Our journey through scripture and hymnody over the last couple of weeks has reminded us of the scale of the battle fought and won. Christ has fought, and God gives us the victory through him.

The last two lines of the hymn present a powerful metaphor, combined with a wordplay involving 'Sun' and 'Son'. During a solar eclipse, the moon moves in front of the sun. It is a dramatic and frightening phenomenon. Similarly, a blood-red sunset sky can touch our emotions at a very deep level. The ancients feared that one day the sun would fall into the sea, never to rise again. The Son's descent into Hades should have been final, and indeed it was. Yet descent was followed by ascent—resurrection. This Sun has risen once more and will never set.

Guidelines

A death-blow is a life-blow to some
Who, till they died, did not alive become;
Who, had they lived, had died, but when
They died, vitality begun.

FROM *SELECTED POEMS*, EMILY DICKINSON (1830–86)

Dickinson's words are no less relevant today than when she composed them well over 100 years ago. Take time to reflect on how these lines connect with this week's readings and with your own experience. Death is never a cause for celebration, but it can be a gateway to life. This week we have been reminded that our Christian lives begin with death—death to self and sin. There is a sense in which we need to die daily in order to become more fully alive, and there is an inevitability of physical death as a journey all must travel. The only one who did not need to pass through death to enter into life was Christ himself. Yet he chose to do so, and his death is our life begun.

FURTHER READING

Emily Dickinson, *Selected Poems*, Outlet Book Company, 1993.

PHILIPPIANS

You can still see the ruins of Philippi, in northern Greece, a few miles from the Aegean coast. In New Testament times it was a medium-sized town, of a few thousand people. Yet Philippi was an important place. It stood in a strategic site, between the mountains and the sea, spanning the main road from Asia into Europe. A hundred years earlier a major battle had been fought there. Afterwards many retired soldiers were settled in the town, and Philippi was granted a special status. It became a Roman 'colony', a little twin town of the capital of the empire. Privileges and tax breaks went with the honour, many local people were Roman citizens, and there was a keen sense of loyalty to Rome.

Philippi was important in the early Christian movement, too. As Paul's missionary journeys took him westward, this was the first bridgehead of the faith in Greece. Acts 16 tells how the gospel came there, and a turbulent tale it is. This church had faced persecution, almost from day one. But they had survived as a fellowship, and later sent money to Paul, to support him in his preaching elsewhere.

So Philippians is a note of thanks for a gift gratefully received. It is also a word of encouragement to a people under pressure. Paul himself is in prison (1:12–13), and he has heard about suffering at Philippi too (1:27–30). His letter is a lifeline, from one who understands, and in it are the two key ingredients of pastoral theology. There is plenty of personal experience—Paul's own, the Philippians', and a few lines about people they both know. And there is a solid anchor in the gospel story, in the life, death and resurrection of Jesus. He is the Church's inspiration and example, the template and target for Christians under strain. 'Christ Jesus has made me his own,' says Paul, 'and I press on to gain Christ and know Christ' (3:8–12).

Paul wrote pastorally, but also carefully. One of the recognized skills of his day was rhetoric, the art of presenting a message, in speaking or in writing. This letter shows some of the typical patterns of rhetoric—not to camouflage the message, but to make it clear. If the readers could grasp the message, they might be grasped afresh by Christ. For Philippians is full of Christ—of death and life, of pain and joy, of distress and of glad hope.

These notes are mainly based on the New Revised Standard Version.

1 Friends in the faith

Philippians 1:1–11

Paul's greeting, in the first two verses, shows what binds writer and readers together. Jesus is the glue of their relationship. This letter is about life lived 'in Christ Jesus', and about people who are linked to God through all that Jesus has done. In Christ ministers are servants and Christians are saints, a people holy to the Lord (v. 1). God is gracious. And true peace comes from Jesus, to hold his people steady and secure, even when their outward circumstances are unsettled and uncertain (v. 2).

Paul's letters often start with a prayer (vv. 3–11), which sets the tone for the message to come. Here the chief notes are thanksgiving and hope. Paul is grateful for all that he and the Philippians have 'shared', for the experiences that join his life to theirs. When he says 'sharing in the gospel' (v. 5), he surely remembers the gifts they have sent to support his mission. He feels they share in his suffering too (v. 7). Their friendship helps to sustain him in prison. Perhaps he will have to defend himself in court, but he knows that they too are standing up for the faith in a testing environment. He and they are linked.

So Paul gives thanks. He is glad to think of his friends in Philippi, and his heart goes out to them as he writes (vv. 3, 4, 8). Even busy people need friends and, when life is tough, it means a lot when friends take trouble to care, to write or to help. The Philippians have helped Paul, and they have lifted his spirits. It gives him confidence to hear that they are holding the faith. God is still at work in them.

So Paul looks ahead. He can trust God to look after his friends, to support the church in Philippi until 'the day of Christ Jesus' (v. 6). That is the final horizon, when God will draw together all he has begun. As Paul looks forward, he asks not just that the Church survive. He wants his friends to grow, in love and in knowledge (vv. 9–11). Then their lives will be fruitful and true. They will have the wisdom to make good choices in a complex world, and to come clean and forgiven to God's last day.

2 Cell church

Philippians 1:12–18

Philippians was written in prison, but we do not know where. Most probably Paul wrote this letter during the period described at the very end of Acts. He had been taken to Rome for trial, and he was kept under house arrest for two years, with a soldier watching him. Now word had got around the garrison that this was a man of faith. His offence was religious. Even the hard soldiers of the imperial guard knew.

The Christians in the city heard about Paul's imprisonment, too. For most of them, Paul's experience had strengthened their witness. His willingness to suffer gave them courage too, to declare their faith openly, to be known for their beliefs and to spread the gospel. Many of them tried to support him, by carrying on the work he was not free to do.

But there was also a response of another kind. For the church in Rome in this period was quite a mixed company, and Paul himself was a strong-minded and controversial character. Not all of the Christians there liked what they knew about him. Indeed some of them saw his imprisonment as an opportunity to gain ground for their version of the gospel, or for their particular section of the church.

So two groups of Christians were active, but with different motives in mind. Understandably, Paul praises one group and criticizes the other. But even when he speaks of his rivals, his main concern is not criticism; it is Christ. 'What does it matter?' he says, 'Christ is proclaimed... and in that I rejoice' (v. 18).

This note of joy crops up all through Philippians. Paul's spirit was light, even though his outward circumstances were burdensome. He was able to think positively, not simply as a mental exercise, but as a natural outflow of his faith. This positive outlook helped him to be a credible Christian witness, when he was under severe pressure. It enabled him, too, to bear with a divided and disputatious church, and still to affirm all they were doing for the sake of Christ. The gospel matters, more than any of our separate Christian interests.

3 In the face of death

Philippians 1:18b–26

Paul is shut in, but his spirit is free. He may die, but he knows he will live, with Christ. The future is uncertain, but he is confident and determined. There is a trial ahead, and he will have to defend himself, yet he is not afraid. What matters to him above all is that he honour Christ, either by living as a Christian or by dying for his faith.

Paul speaks as if he has a decision to make, a path to choose. If he lives, he can go on working. He can support the churches who rely on his leadership and experience. His friends will be glad to see him again, and he will be able to achieve something for the gospel. On the other hand, if he dies, he will 'depart and be with Christ' (v. 23), which will be 'far better' for him. It may be that Paul actually had some choice about the kind of legal defence he could offer. If he were silent in court, as Jesus had been, he could expect martyrdom. If he defended himself, there was some prospect of release. But he could scarcely have been certain of the outcome, and if he needs to die, he is ready.

Some writers in the ancient world thought of death as a welcome escape from a tired and demeaning world. But this is not Paul's view. When death comes, he wants to welcome it as a positive step, into the presence of his Lord. Christ's grasp on us will not weaken when we die. Death will take us closer to him. It is good to die as a Christian, and Paul longs for this, but he will not do anything to hasten it or bring it on himself. Indeed he wants and expects to live on. Friends have prayed for him, the churches need him, and he is confident that he will be spared to carry God's work forward. He has a strong sense of call, and he trusts God to keep him alive until his work is done.

This passage has helped many Christians to face death with a clear and calm mind. Certainly we should value the life God has given, and expect God to use us for as long as we live. But when our time comes, death is a gift of God and a door into the presence of Christ. We need not fear.

4 Firm and faithful

Philippians 1:27—2:4

Many writers or speakers in the ancient world would follow a regular pattern for setting out what they had to say. First, give some personal news, show that you have a right to speak and that you have a bond with your hearers. Paul has done this through most of Philippians 1. Next, state your main point, as Paul does here: 'Live a life marked by the gospel, stand firm under pressure, guard your unity' (v. 27). The central part of the speech—Paul's middle two chapters—would explain and expound this point. A summing up might recall the main theme: 'stand firm... be of one mind' (4:1–2). Then finally the speech would move towards a conclusion.

Paul, it seems, is using this sort of pattern, and the short paragraph at the end of Philippians 1 is the so-called 'proposition', the summary of his pastoral advice to this church. They were coping with pressure and opposition, and Paul uses the language of the battlefield to encourage them: 'stand, strive, struggle'. They must be as solid as an army unit under attack. Yet military language has its limits. Paul does not tell these Christians to be aggressive, simply to be steady and strong.

Strength depends on two virtues, on courage and on mutual care. Paul surely thinks that his personal example can help the Philippians to be brave. That is one reason he has written about his difficulties (1:12–26). But unity is important too, and it is a major emphasis of these verses: 'one spirit... one mind' (v. 27); 'a common mind, love and attitude' (2:2). When there is pressure from outside, the church can only be steady if there is strength on the inside, and if people look out for one another. Living by the gospel must involve loving attitudes, expressed in the piecemeal pattern of daily contact and concern (v. 4).

For Paul, Christianity is both practical and corporate: we live it together. The belief that Christians share, and the Spirit who binds us together, draw the church into a gospel-shaped way of living. Humility, service and love are the marks of this lifestyle. And the template is Jesus Christ himself, about whom we hear much more in the verses ahead.

5 The mind of Christ

Philippians 2:5–11

Verses 6 to 11 are famous. Sometimes they are referred to as 'the Christ-hymn', because Paul's writing has suddenly become lyrical and even rhythmic. Some Bibles lay out this portion of Philippians as if it were poetry. Perhaps, it is said, this was a piece of early Christian praise, which the Philippians would know well. That might be why Paul uses it, just as a preacher today might quote a well-known hymn, to make a practical point.

Whoever composed this piece, it fits very well within Paul's letter. Verse 5 links it to what has gone before. Bear up under pressure, Paul has said, by nurturing your unity (1:27–30): care for each other, and live humbly (2:1–4). Aim to have a common attitude to life, and be 'of one mind' (v. 2). The only sure way to achieve this is to adopt 'the mind of Christ' (v. 5). He is our model and example of a life offered in humble service to God and others.

Jesus was 'in the form of God' (v. 6). This word 'form' means more than outward shape or appearance. It is the essence and nature of a thing. So Paul thinks of Jesus as genuinely one with God, before he took our flesh—before Bethlehem, we might say. Yet Jesus did not cling to this dignity. He became powerless, humble and human. He 'emptied himself' (v. 7), by pouring himself into a lowly role, into 'the form of a slave'. And again the word 'form' means that Jesus was truly one who served. He was not simply acting a part, but being himself, when he lived and died as one of us.

In Jesus we see that God's nature is a servant nature. God is generous, humble, self-giving. The crucifixion does not rub out the face of God; it shows that face to the world. Love and service, action and compassion, are the way God is. This is the life to which we are called, as we follow Jesus our leader, and share his outlook on God's world.

6 Name above all names

(Re-read) Philippians 2:5–11

As so often in the New Testament, there are hints and echoes of several Old Testament passages in this 'Christ-hymn'. Some people have overheard the story of Adam in these lines. He reached too high, in an attempt to get level with God, and then fell heavily, to live as a creature of dust and defeat. Philippians 2, of course, turns that story upside down. Jesus is a new Adam, who stoops low, and surrenders his privilege (vv. 6–8). Then God honours and vindicates what he has done. He is raised high, to be covered with glory and praise (vv. 9–11). The second Adam reverses the pattern of the first, and brings a new kind of humanity into being, a family of people whose lives reflect his.

There is another resonance, when we read of Jesus coming in the 'form of a slave' (v. 7). In the prophecy of Isaiah is a figure called the Servant of God (52:13—53:12). He suffers, to bring blessing and hope to many, and then he is raised high. Paul certainly uses this text elsewhere, and it may have been in his mind as he wrote Philippians.

A stronger echo of Isaiah comes in verses 9–11. 'To me every knee shall bow, and every tongue swear,' says Israel's Lord, 'for I am God and there is no other' (45:22–23). The 'name that is above every name', given to the risen and ascended Jesus, is the name of the God of Israel. 'Jesus Christ is Lord.' The rank and position he receives reveal him as one with God—not as a competitor or companion to God, but someone who shares and expresses the very life of God, as ruler of heaven and earth.

So finally the hymn returns to heaven, like a great parabola, reaching down to the cross and curving back to the heights. It is praise, and practical too, speaking directly to Christians in Philippi. Jesus' humility is a model for them to follow. God has honoured this way of life, and will surely honour it still. Amid the pressures of their situation, in a proud and well-connected town, they may look to Jesus, who is Lord of all God's worlds. True glory belongs to the one who came as Servant, died in weakness and rose in power.

Guidelines

Philippians links the story of Jesus to the situation of a troubled and struggling church. Paul reminds his friends, and reminds us too, that Christian belief makes a difference in practice. It helps Christians to live as a people 'of one mind', with an attitude of care and respect for each other. It gives the church unity and strength under pressure. It inspires us to be generous, and helps us feel close to one another, even when we are apart or alone. And it gives courage in the face of death. When we sing or speak of our belief in church, when we remember the faith we hold, it is good to recall too that this faith holds and sustains us, in the fellowship and love of Jesus.

1 We can work it out?

Philippians 2:12–18

'Work out your own salvation' (v. 12) may sound like spiritual DIY ('do it yourself'), and Paul certainly wants his friends to put some effort into their Christian living. They have to do it. But not alone, nor in their own strength. The only sure way to put faith into practice is by God's strength and wisdom. And God is at work in his people, shaping desire and deed to the pattern of his will (v. 13).

Paul knows that he cannot help the Philippians from a distance as well as if he were there (v. 12). Yet he is still acutely aware of the bonds and relationships that link him to this church. He feels that they and he suffer together. His sacrificial commitment to God is all of a piece with theirs, and this makes him glad, with them and over them (v. 17). He looks forward in hope. All that he does and bears will be worthwhile, if they keep the faith (v. 16).

Paul's train of thought often seems influenced by the Old Testament. 'Murmuring and arguing' (v. 14) was an exodus chorus, as the Israelites trudged wearily through the desert. Yet Paul's message recalls Moses' last speech to Israel, at the end of that journey. God can be trusted, even when times have been hard and leaders are far away (Deuteronomy 31:6, 8). The thought that Christians 'shine like stars' (v. 15) echoes Daniel (12:3). They will be beacons, to lead others into right habits of life, even when the world seems a murky and mixed-up place.

'Working out our salvation' is never a task for Christians to do alone. The goodness and guidance of God are engine and compass for the journey. The warnings and promises of scripture light the way and lead us on. The fellowship of Christians far and near, many of them facing the same struggles we do, is encouragement and joy. And the hope that our life will count, in the clear light of God's last judgment, stirs and sustains us. Philippians was written in a time of suffering and stress. Paul and his friends knew what he was talking about. When our resources fail, God's will not.

2 Our mutual friends

Philippians 2:19–30

Teachers know the importance of giving examples. If people see an idea working in practice, it will lodge more securely in everybody's mind. Pastors know the value of staying in contact. When you keep lines of communication open, as well as you can, you will support and nurture people much more effectively. Here we see Paul following both of these principles. He cannot come to Philippi himself, but he keeps in touch by sending messengers and helpers. And as he writes about Christian values and lifestyle, he talks of two people who put these standards into action.

These two men were well known to the readers of the letter, as well as to Paul. Timothy was Paul's assistant for many years. They had started travelling together before they first came to Philippi (Acts 16:3, 12), so the people there would have known him over some years. Epaphroditus belonged to Philippi, and was sent by the church to bring gifts to Paul and to offer him help (2:25, 30; 4:18). Now it was time for Paul to send him home, carrying this letter.

So Paul wants to thank the church in Philippi for the help Epaphroditus has given, and to praise the attitude he has shown. We do not know what his illness was, but it was clearly serious, as illnesses often were in the ancient world, and it had almost cost his life (vv. 27, 30). Yet all along he was more concerned for others than for himself—the sort of friend anyone would appreciate, and a fine example of the teaching just given. He has 'regarded others as better than himself' (v. 3), and served without murmur or question (v. 14).

Timothy, too, looks to the interests of others, rather than his own (vv. 4, 21), and he stayed loyal to Paul (v. 22) when others pursued their separate rivalries and ambitions (1:17). He is someone Paul can trust with an important pastoral errand, and he will come to Philippi as soon as he is available. Then when Timothy reports back, Paul expects to be 'cheered' by his news (v. 19). Despite prison, illness, opposition, uncertainty and distance, this letter is full of joy (v. 29). Joy of this kind is a gift from God, and a taste of the risen life of Jesus Christ.

3 Value judgment

Philippians 3:1–11

'Rejoice in the Lord' (v. 1) is a value judgment. Paul believes that the surest and deepest kind of happiness finds its support and centre in the Lord Jesus. He found this centre in his own life, but he also had to review and revalue some things that once made him very proud. Now he wants his friends in Philippi to reflect about their values, and about what really matters to them.

The people Paul warns against (v. 2) were probably not local to Philippi. There had been some local opposition (1:27–30), and it first arose because the Christians were seen as a disruptive and counter-cultural lot: they were not Roman enough (Acts 16:20). But the 'flesh-cutters' whom Paul mentions (v. 2) had different concerns. They saw Gentile Christians as not Jewish enough, and they wanted to make them more truly Jewish (they might have said), by circumcising the men among them. Paul's warning here seems precautionary rather than urgent. The people he mentions were probably not in Philippi at the moment. But to help his readers think about the issues, Paul tells his own story.

He himself had plenty of advantages—birth, breeding, background (vv. 4–6). But knowing Christ put all of these in a different light. Paul talks of this change in four ways. First is the language of book-keeping and accountancy, of profit and loss (vv. 7–8). Next he talks of 'rubbish', an old pride that is cleared out, so that his life can be gathered into the life of Christ (vv. 8–9). Then he mentions 'law' and 'faith', and explains that he has moved from one to the other, as the basis of his relationship with God (v. 9). Finally he turns to crucifixion and resurrection, the events that shaped the gospel, which have now become the goal and inspiration of his own journey (vv. 10–11).

Paul's own readiness to set privilege aside resonates deeply with the story of Jesus (2:6), who chose a servant life above everything else. Jesus' story is the pattern, the original, for the path Christians follow in his name. It is no surprise, then, when following him leads to suffering (v. 10). Yet within the suffering is the power of resurrection, of new life and hope, even in places of pressure and death.

4 Running for heaven

Philippians 3:12–21

Many people in the ancient Greek world took sport and fitness seriously, and New Testament letters often use the language of the athletic track as a picture of the Christian life. 'Pressing towards the goal, reaching for the prize'—this is Paul's description of his own attitude (vv. 13–14). Now that he knows Jesus, he does not settle for an easy life, as if his journey is complete. But the full glory of resurrection is ahead of him, and he lives as someone whose eyes are firmly on the future. Christians taste Easter now, but our full and final hope is 'resurrection from the dead' (v. 11), and the 'heavenly call of God' (v. 14). Hope quickens the step, and sustains us till the road is done.

For Paul, the Christian life is a strenuous and serious business. It takes effort, stamina and purpose. Yet in a strange way, it does not depend on effort alone. 'I press on,' says Paul, 'because Christ Jesus has made me his own' (v. 12). We saw the same pattern earlier (2:12–13): God is at work, and this means that we too can work, energetically and confidently. So Paul urges the Christians in Philippi to press ahead. He gives four reasons to spur them on.

First, it is a mark of maturity to know that you have not arrived spiritually (v. 15). Next, having started on the Christian road, they should keep going and not waste the progress they have made (v. 16). Thirdly, they should be wary of the kind of life that lacks all spiritual vision, as if earth were all there is (vv. 18–19). Finally, they should realize that they already belong to heaven. They can look forward to the time when heaven enfolds the life of earth, and our mortal flesh is caught up completely by the glory of resurrection (vv. 20–21).

This last idea, about 'citizenship in heaven', would have a particular meaning in Philippi. This was a 'colony', a little outpost of Rome.

Though a distant and smallish city, it was linked by law and privilege to the great centre of imperial rule and power. In the same way the church at Philippi was an outpost of heaven, a colony of people who belonged to God's kingdom. They could run with hope, even when the road was hard and heaven seemed far away.

5 Pressures and priorities

Philippians 4:1–9

'Stand firm,' says Paul (v. 1). We have heard this message before (1:27), and the central chapters of his letter have been method and motivation for acting on it. Today's verses round off Paul's practical advice, and from 4:10 onwards he will turn again to personal news. But before that, he speaks about the qualities of fellowship and of personality that will help the Philippians to 'stand firm'.

We know nothing about Euodia and Syntyche, apart from these few words here. We may guess that they belonged to the little group around Lydia, where the gospel had first taken hold in Philippi (Acts 16:13–15). They worked hard to keep the faith and to share it (v. 3). Then it appears that some difficulty or dispute arose between them. Even good church workers can get worn down by tiredness, or tangled in misunderstandings. Yet quarrels that we cannot mend will weaken the fellowship around us. It is hard to stand firm under pressure, when key people are at odds with each other.

'Please help them,' says Paul to his mysterious 'loyal companion' (v. 3). It is possible this could be Luke, whose 'we' passages in Acts sometimes begin or end at Philippi (16:17: 20:5). Maybe Luke belonged to Philippi, or at least spent time with the church there. Certainly this 'companion' would have a vital support role, as Euodia and Syntyche worked through their troubles.

To live the faith well, Christians need one another. We also need to work at our individual character and habits of life. Times may have felt very unstable for the Philippians, yet Paul talks about steady and settled attitudes, about the 'peace of God' and the 'God of peace' (vv. 7, 9). Focus on what is worthy and true (v. 8), he says. Follow good leadership (v. 9), remember God's closeness (v. 5), and take time to pray (v. 6). This helps to keep the spirit buoyant and the mind calm, with peace and joy that we can never fully fathom (vv. 4, 7).

The virtues Paul lists (v. 8) were valued by many Greek thinkers. Paul did sometimes use language and ideas that his readers had heard elsewhere. Yet what he wrote earlier about 'the mind of Christ' (2:5) gives Christians example and energy when we aim at these habits of life. We never tackle these tasks alone, but 'in the Lord', as people who trust and follow Jesus.

6 Giving, greetings and grace

Philippians 4:10–23

At the very start of the letter, Paul wrote of the Philippians 'sharing in the gospel' (1:5). They had sent him gifts by the hand of Epaphroditus, and in these last few verses Paul thanks them. Yet he never actually says 'thank you', and there may be a good reason for this. In the Greek and Roman world, gifts and giving were part of a complex web of social convention, and were often linked to issues of status, influence, rank and power. So Paul avoids the direct language of social custom. He does not want the Philippians to misunderstand their relationship with him. Instead he explains fully, carefully and gratefully just how he feels about the Philippians' gift. He wants them to see that, for Christians, giving is a spiritual act—a response to God, rather than an attempt to influence people.

So Paul writes of joy (v. 10), of the Philippians' kindness in his distress (v. 14), and of their long record of support for his ministry (vv. 15–16). He thinks of their generosity to him as an offering, as worship that will delight and honour God (v. 18). They will gain and grow from their giving (v. 17). It will be a 'profit' to them, helping them forward on the Christian way.

Yet as Paul rejoices, he recalls harder times that have afflicted him. There have been seasons of poverty, need and hunger, and as God has sustained him, Paul has learned to trust. However dark or dire the situation, God can handle it, and Paul can face it in God's strength (vv. 11–13). So he reminds his friends that God will support and sustain them too (v. 19). They are in good hands.

Finally Paul signs off, with words of glory, greeting and grace (vv. 20–23). Christians are 'saints' (as in 1:1), a holy people with a commitment to godly living, wherever we go in the world. Even at this early stage in the Church's history, Christians were found in unexpected places, including some in 'the emperor's household' (v. 22). Whatever their job—and this we don't know at all—these people seem to have worked in a centre of power. Yet when he calls them 'saints', Paul reminds all his readers that whoever our earthly employer is, we should always aim to serve in the mind and spirit of Christ.

Guidelines

Philippians is about people—Euodia and Epaphroditus, Syntyche and Timothy, Paul and a church he loved dearly. It is full of affection and honest advice, and it makes very clear that Christians belong together. We need each other. We often learn the faith best by copying one another, by following good examples, and by giving of ourselves and our substance when there is hurt or need.

Philippians is about Jesus. The 'Christ-hymn' in chapter 2 is a pattern for our service, for our relationships and for our Christian journey. The Church is a community, centred on Jesus Christ, as a leader to follow and a Lord to trust.

Philippians is honest about hardship: about prison and the prospect of death, about poverty and illness, about anxiety and opposition, and about divisions in the Church. The early Christians were a vulnerable community and sometimes a troubled one. The gospel may not spare us difficulty, but it can sustain us as we meet it.

Finally, Philippians is about rejoicing and joy, seeping into and out of almost every corner of the letter. Joy seems to have come naturally to Paul. Friendship quickened his spirit. He loved people, for Jesus' sake, and he loved telling them about the faith. There was a joy in following Jesus, and there still is.

FURTHER READING

G.B. Caird, *Paul's Letters from Prison* (New Clarendon Bible: Oxford University Press, 1976). A small commentary, with much wisdom and detail. Covers Ephesians, Colossians and Philemon too.

G.D. Fee, *Paul's Letter to the Philippians* (New International Commentary: Eerdmans, 1995). A big commentary—weighty, learned, careful and clear.

S.E. Fowl, *Philippians* (Two Horizons New Testament Commentary: Eerdmans, 2005). A medium-sized book, with a lively interest in the letter's teaching about God, and about the Christian life.

The BRF

Magazine

Order forms

Richard Fisher writes...

A 'fellowship' is a group of people who come together to share a particular aim or interest, who take pleasure in each other's company and in the goals they have in common. At BRF, the Bible Reading Fellowship, we are well aware of the benefits of this sharing, as the staff team works together to produce Bible reading notes and books, and as the Barnabas ministry team pool their creativity and expertise to inspire the pupils, teachers and children's workers they meet through the year.

We also know how encouraging it is to have other people around us to share our spiritual journey. So in this issue of the BRF Magazine, Ceri Ellis, who is part of our Marketing team, sets out the advantages of reading regularly as a group of subscribers, while Tony Horsfall writes on his work as a mentor and retreat leader, accompanying others in their walk with God.

One central aspect of fellowship is sharing meals together, and two of our contributors in this issue take food as their theme. First comes an extract from this year's Lent book, *Fasting and Feasting* by Gordon Giles, and then Margaret Withers writes about how to involve the whole congregation in Holy Communion, the meal that defines our fellowship with Jesus Christ and with other believers.

Within those congregations, children are an important but often neglected part of our fellowship. At BRF we have a burgeoning ministry among children, and Jane Butcher, the *Barnabas* team member based in the Midlands, explains part of her role, bringing the Bible alive in schools. We would be delighted if you were inspired by her report to join in the work in whatever way you can.

Finally, *New Daylight* editor Naomi Starkey reminds us that our discipleship involves, first and foremost, drawing closer to God, who is active in the world of human beings and loves to work in fellowship with us. Naomi recommends two BRF books that encourage us to collaborate with God and other people in the work to which he calls us.

Thank you for your continued prayers for BRF. We very much appreciate your 'partnership in the gospel' (Philippians 1:5).

Richard Fisher, Chief Executive

Sharing in the Bible together

Ceri Ellis

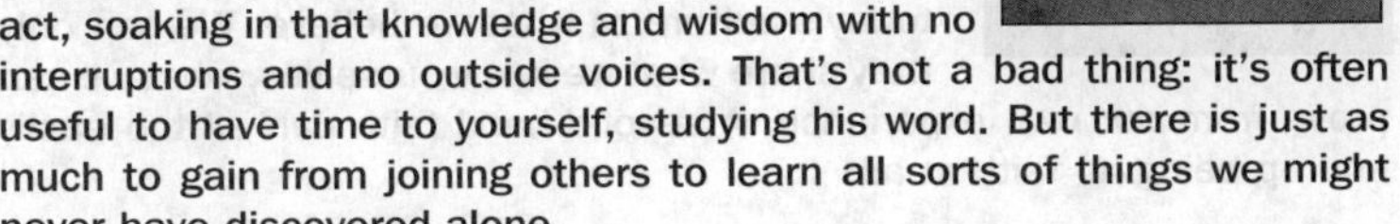

Some people prefer to read the Bible as a solitary act, soaking in that knowledge and wisdom with no interruptions and no outside voices. That's not a bad thing: it's often useful to have time to yourself, studying his word. But there is just as much to gain from joining others to learn all sorts of things we might never have discovered alone.

Everyone has a different insight on a favourite verse or a less well understood chapter; suddenly the Bible becomes richer, multifaceted, and our understanding is deepened. And all this through time spent with friends! In the BRF offices, we read *New Daylight* together every morning, and I always appreciate the words even more just because of the presence of others and the fellowship we share.

At BRF, we are keen to encourage you to spend more time with the Bible and with each other. The group subscription system is a great way to do that. By gathering a minimum of five people subscribing to a mix of any of our Bible reading notes (*New Daylight*, *Guidelines* and *Day by Day with God*) or our prayer and spirituality journal *Quiet Spaces*, you can be classified as a group. What's so great about being in a group? Not only do you get the chance to experience the Bible with your fellow churchgoers or cell group, but you also qualify for a discount on the individual subscription rate, as you do not have to pay postage. With a rolling subscription system, you won't have to renew anything with us: just let us know if you want to change the number of copies you receive.

You'll be pleasantly surprised at the difference four extra heads make when looking at a particular Bible passage. So why not give the groups system a try? Perhaps it will enrich your spiritual life; perhaps it will strengthen your relationships with the people around you. It may even do both! If you would like to start a group in your local area, please phone me on 01865 319709 or email ceri.ellis@brf.org.uk, and I will be happy to start you off on the process.

To compare our individual and group subscription rates, *see page 157.*

The Editor recommends

Naomi Starkey

The path of Christian discipleship involves both learning more about God—drawing closer to him—and learning more about how we witness in today's culture to what we believe. We can only truly share what we know ourselves, what we can prove from our own experience. A second-hand faith can all too easily end up being no faith at all.

Two recent books published by BRF, *Into Your Hands* and *Growing Women Leaders*, present contrasting and at the same time complementary perspectives on these issues. Both combine an emphasis on knowing what we believe and why with the importance of expressing our beliefs clearly to the watching world.

Kevin Scully's *Into Your Hands* explores what it means to say that God is at work in the world today—specifically, how the hand of God can interact with the actions of human beings, who are themselves acting as 'God's hands' as they go about their daily lives. Beginning with creation and moving on to reflect on the person and work of Jesus, the book considers how God—Father, Son, Spirit—has worked and continues to work to shape the events of history. It also considers how individuals, communities and churches might respond. The concluding section focuses on the events of Jesus' death and resurrection, his broken hands outstretched to bring healing and salvation, as the mystery of redemption unfolds.

Each chapter concludes with questions for discussion or individual reflection, meditative exercises and a prayer. In a foreword warmly endorsing the book, John Sentamu, Archbishop of York, writes, '*Into Your Hands* points to the way God has given us life in his created order and new life in Jesus. It also reminds us that there is a practical working out of our faith. We cannot but want to put our hands on the plough. After all, the future is in our hands as God's invited guests and friends.'

Author Kevin Scully has also written *Sensing the Passion* and *Women on the Way* (both published by Triangle/SPCK), as well as contributing to a number of other books. Ordained in the Church of England, he has served his entire ministry in inner-city London and is currently the rector of St Matthew's, Bethnal Green, in the East End. A former actor and journalist, he has also written ten produced stage works and two radio plays.

By contrast, *Growing Women Leaders* examines a specific issue in the life of the Church (and, by extension, in society in general). As the title states, this is a book about women's leadership in the Church, considering the current situation and looking to the future.

As the years have passed since the Church of England decided to ordain women to the priesthood, it is tempting to assume that the debate on whether women should lead at all is now over. Author Rosie Ward shows, however, that there is still more to do for churches to become places where women and men can truly share authority and have the same opportunities to exercise a ministry of leadership.

This is not just a matter of church policy but of discipleship. Rosie Ward surveys the latest scholarship on key scripture passages relating to women leaders, outlines the long history of women in church leadership, and offers much practical advice on helping women grow as leaders. While avoiding stereotypes, she argues that women have unique gifts to bring to leadership and that they need targeted help to nurture these gifts. If the Church does not utilize women in leadership, not only is their potential untapped but everybody is impoverished.

The book is written to inspire and nurture women already in leadership, as well as encouraging those exploring a call to this ministry. It is also essential reading for men—all those who work alongside women leaders in the Church and those involved in the selection and training of women for ministry.

Rosie Ward works with the Church Pastoral Aid Society (CPAS), with a particular brief for developing women as leaders in the Church. She is also involved with CPAS's vocations work, encouraging people to consider church ministry. She previously spent eleven years in parish ministry herself, has written *Liberating Women for the Gospel* and three Grove booklets, and has also contributed to *The Church of England Newspaper*, *Ministry Today*, *Women Alive* and *Anvil*.

In Hebrews 13, we find a prayer for all believers, that 'the God of peace [may]... equip you with everything good for doing his will' (vv. 20–21, TNIV). As we grow in stature as disciples, we will find ourselves equipped for the tasks to which God calls us in his world. It is my prayer that these two books, in their different ways, will provide help in this process for all who read them.

To order a copy of Into Your Hands *or* Growing Women Leaders, *please turn to the order form on page 159.*

An extract from *Fasting and Feasting*

We know that food and drink are fundamental to life, yet how many of us have ever thought about what the Bible has to say on the subject? BRF's Lent book for 2009, by *New Daylight* contributor Gordon Giles, takes food as its focus. The Lenten fast concludes with the Easter feast, and, in between, *Fasting and Feasting* examines a range of issues from hospitality to our stewardship of the world's resources. This abridged extract is taken from the first two readings in the book.

Shrove Tuesday

We cannot overemphasize the influence of Jewish tradition on the Christian faith, and nowhere is it more prevalent than in the various rituals and attitudes we have with regard to our food. The central rite of the Christian faith, the Eucharist, owes a tremendous amount to the Passover feast, from which it evolved. Our approach to feasting is hardly a Christian invention and the flipside, the fast, also has origins in Jewish practice. As we embark on a food tourist's journey through Lent, we will surely find ourselves spending time at the tables of both Passover and Holy Communion. We will also find ourselves examining tables today and questioning our relationship with food in this day and age. While climate change often steals the headlines, recent government health warnings against obesity suggest that it is as great a problem, yet at the same time many people strive to obtain the slim figure of a supermodel and eat very little. In obscene contrast, the populations of some nations starve. It is no longer obvious that food is always a blessing, and it is timely to consider food as a multidimensional aspect of today's economical, physical and spiritual life.

Before we begin, it is Shrove Tuesday, the spiritual equivalent of the day before the morning after! … Shrove Tuesday is not really a feast day as such. It is rather a day prior to a fast day, which is not quite the same thing. Its very name speaks of repentance rather than indulgence and it is good to remember that, while the aroma of maple syrup and pancakes wafts heavenward. 'Shrove' comes from the old English word 'shrive', which means to impose a penance.

Thus it was the priest's role to 'shrive' a person: to hear their confession, allocate them penance to amend for their sins and to pronounce God's forgiveness. To be 'shriven' is to have made one's confession and been absolved. The Reformation theologians were rightly concerned about the potential abuses of a mechanistic approach to forgiveness, especially where money changed hands, but it is ironic that Shrove Tuesday is now more associated with gluttony than penitence. Originally, the period from the Sunday before Ash Wednesday... through to the Tuesday was known as 'Shrovetide' and Christians were expected to make confession and receive absolution, in preparation for the great fast of Lent that begins tomorrow.

During that fast, comestibles such as meat, sweet things, fatty food, sauces or anything apparently extravagant would be abandoned until the Easter feast. This tradition is still very much alive, manifesting itself when people give up chocolate or alcohol for Lent. Early tradition also gives us the threefold discipline of prayer (justice towards God), fasting (justice towards self), and almsgiving (justice towards others). The use of the Gloria at the Mass, and Allelluias, were dropped in Lent, and a general feel of austerity was cultivated. Another devotional tradition also developed, in which this very book stands. Early Christian converts went through a process of instruction prior to baptism during the Lent season (in fact, that is how we acquired Lent in the first place). This was a discipline not only of self-denial but of learning, and the idea of reading books for Lent has descended from that desire for knowledge and truth, so that when Easter Day comes we are not only purer but more knowledgeable about the faith we profess and celebrate. St Benedict declared in his Rule that reading and study were important for any monk, but especially in Lent, when each day a book should be read 'straight through'.

It is in the spirit of this tradition that I offer you this volume, not so much to be read straight through but to be tasted daily, rather like a journey around the table of the Bible, or like a 46-course banquet. Each day's 'plate' will complement the others while, I hope, being tasty on its own... In Lent it is good to taste and see the goodness of the Lord, perhaps in a different way, bringing out different or new flavours. This year, try a biblical diet of feasting as well as fasting, in which we shall consider passages that are either obviously or subtly about food or drink, or about the Eucharist, or that point us forward to the heavenly banquet to which our Lord Jesus Christ invites each and every one of us.

So as we fast and feast together this Lent, it remains only for me to wish you *bon appetit*!

Ash Wednesday

Yet even now, says the Lord, return to me with all your heart, with fasting, with weeping, and with mourning; rend your hearts and not your clothing. Return to the Lord, your God, for he is gracious and merciful, slow to anger, and abounding in steadfast love, and relents from punishing. Who knows whether he will not turn and relent, and leave a blessing behind him, a grain-offering and a drink-offering for the Lord, your God? Blow the trumpet in Zion; sanctify a fast; call a solemn assembly; gather the people. Sanctify the congregation; assemble the aged; gather the children, even infants at the breast. Let the bridegroom leave his room, and the bride her canopy. Between the vestibule and the altar let the priests, the ministers of the Lord, weep. Let them say, 'Spare your people, O Lord, and do not make your heritage a mockery, a byword among the nations.'

JOEL 2:12–17

We saw yesterday how the traditions of Shrovetide have their origins in medieval confession and absolution; there are also similarities to Jewish Passover ritual. As we begin Lent, this passage from Joel is read in many churches today. In his brief work of prophecy, Joel declares the 'day of the Lord', the day on which God appears in a blaze of glory but also heralds drought, famine and anguish (see 1:15–18; 2:1–2). He calls for a widespread and complete manifestation of repentence: fasting, weeping and mourning. The tradition of tearing clothes as a sign of grief is not enough: it is time to tear our hearts and return to the Lord. Everyone—men, women, the old and the young—is to participate in a communal ritual of fasting and prayer that acknowledges guilt and indicates to God their sincerity and love.

If the people did what Joel proposed, it must have been quite a sight. Just imagine the whole of our nation or community united in penitence or sorrow for sin. That would be a real start to Lent, wouldn't it? And it would mark a great contrast with our normal practice: it is hard to get people to come to church on Ash Wednesday, the news media do not mention the significance of the day, and there seems to be just as much sin, pain and grief around as there is on any other day. If people do know about Lent, they do not understand it in the way that Joel understands a general fast. For many, Lent is about 'giving something up', and in this spirit we have created traditions that relate to the spiritual fast of Lent in a physical way. Where there are food traditions for eating up surplus supplies on Shrove Tuesday, there is an inevitable dimension in which we think of future deprivation as inspiring and condoning a little gluttony. It works on a simple level: eat something nice, then deny it to yourself and return to it at the end of the fast, when you will appreciate it all the more. In this way, the spiritual season is physically marked out, but it is very different from what Joel had in mind.

The danger is that the physical dimensions, which are supposed to indicate or underline a spiritual attitude, actually replace it. Lent is not really about 'giving something up'. Giving something up is about Lent. Lent is a period in which we are invited to renew our relationship with God, to 'deny ourselves' and 'take up the cross'. If there is something that comes between us and God, it is good to abandon it in Lent, not only in order to draw closer to God but also to engage in the spiritual discipline of self-denial. There is no point in giving up chocolate, alcohol, sugar, caffeine or some activity if doing so is actually quite easy. Lent is not about what you give up, but about what you do. Sadly, though, over the years, Lent has been perceived negatively as a period for saying 'no', when it is far more challenging and edifying to see it as a period in which we say 'yes' to God as well as 'sorry'. Admittedly, that may involve saying 'no' to ourselves at times.

Fasting is not simply about not eating or giving up certain foods. It is about being humble in the presence of God (Isaiah 58:3–4; Ezra 8:21). The first reference to fasting in the Bible comes when David fasts after his indiscretion with Bathsheba has led to her pregnancy, and he prays that the child may be spared (2 Samuel 12:16). Fasts soon became public events and days of fasting were declared, usually by the elders of the community... Fixed fasts were not very common, except that of the Day of Atonement (Yom Kippur), instituted in Leviticus 16:29, which was the fast that hindered Paul's journey to Rome (Acts 27:9). Later, fixed fasts were declared, as in Zechariah 8:19, after the temple was destroyed.

There are two fixed fasts in the Christian calendar. One is today and the other is Good Friday. Flanking Lent for hundreds of years, they are just as useful and relevant today as they ever have been. Many today will receive the imposition of ashes on their foreheads as a mark of penitence—an outward sign of the inward grace of forgiveness granted by God, through the saving work of Christ on the cross, to his faithful people in this faithless and sinful age. Thus it is today that we begin Lent, with humility in our hearts, prayers on our lips and ashes on our heads.

Lord Christ, may we remember that we are dust, and to dust we shall return. Help us turn away from sin to be faithful to you. Amen

To order a copy of this book, please turn to the order form on page 159.

Exploring Holy Communion creatively

Margaret Withers

Imagine a family gathered around the table for supper. It is a special meal: candles are lit, food is enjoyed, wine is drunk and news is shared. Suddenly the youngest child turns to his father. 'Why is tonight different from other nights?' he asks. And, as the full moon shines through the window, his father tells the story of how God delivered their ancestors from slavery and led them over the Red Sea to the promised land.

Every Sunday we call to mind a similar story—how Christ saved us from the slavery of sin through his death and resurrection. We recall it during a meal, the meal he gave us on the night he was betrayed, when he promised to be present whenever we break bread and remember him. One story flows from the other—but, for me, there is one flaw. The Jews place a child in the centre. The party is not complete without him and the story is told in response to his eager questions. How tragic that the Western reformed tradition removed children from the Lord's table and told them the story without the wonder and joy of meeting Jesus through his word and sacrament.

When I was a children's adviser, people would ask me, 'Can we bring the children to the Holy Communion service? How can we involve them?' The early 1990s were the heyday of all-age worship. The family service was becoming popular with churches, encouraging congregational participation.

At the same time, another group (of which I was part) was finding ways of making the Eucharist truly inclusive. We took the words of the service and the Bible readings and used sign and symbol, music and drama, colour, light and movement to help people, whatever their age or stage of faith, to worship God with their whole selves. Yet inclusiveness stopped at the altar. Children were not allowed to receive Holy Communion.

But we have moved on! Today, children may be admitted to Holy Communion before confirmation in the Church of England. It is policy in the Methodist Church and common practice in the URC. Stress on the importance of the manner of celebrating the service has encouraged worship that is creative and accessible to all while retaining its sense of the presence of God and beauty of holiness.

In my preparation course, *Welcome to the Lord's Table*, I wrote that if children were present at the Eucharist as communicants, it would change the whole nature of the service. They would be present as of right, rather than being 'allowed' to come in. It was important to review the service and see how it could relate to everyone: if it was not good enough for children, it was probably not good enough for adults, either. If children were admitted to Holy Communion, it was as part of a continuous process that led up to confirmation and beyond. Parents and church leaders needed to help them to grow in their faith and understanding of the significance of Holy Communion as part of their nurture.

It was from this that the idea came for the book *Creative Communion*. Youngsters who had been admitted to Holy Communion at an early age needed to grow in their discernment of the sacrament and how to live it out in their daily lives. My co-author, Tim Sledge, is one of the most creative priests I know, with wonderful flair and imagination. He suggested that, as the Lord made himself known in a meal among friends, we should base the book on the theme of meals and eating together.

Creative Communion is designed in the shape of a letter 'Y'! The stem explores the Eucharist as a four-course meal, with the basic ingredients enhanced by music, drama, colour and movement. It discusses the place of children as part of the worshipping family and as communicants, and the evangelistic angle of the service. The Jews keep an empty place to welcome the stranger to the Passover table. How do Christians welcome the visitors, the enquirers or those on the fringe of society to our meal?

The branches of the 'Y' are two sets of six workshops. Each session explores a part of the service creatively. The all-age programme includes teaching and practical activities, with time for reflection and planning how to incorporate some of the ideas into the Sunday service. The course for youngsters, 'Food, glorious food', focuses on meals, including cooking, eating and discussion on how to live out the eucharistic life in our daily lives at home and in school.

'Can we bring the children to the Holy Communion service? How can we involve them?' These questions are still being asked, but they are easier to answer today. Children can and should be present at the service. Celebrating it creatively does much to give every person an experience of the presence of God, and the youngest may share fully in the Lord's own meal.

To order a copy of Creative Communion, *please turn to page 159.*

Barnabas RE Days

Jane Butcher

'Privilege', 'inspiring', 'challenging', 'fun' and 'tiring' are all words that might be used to describe the experience of a *Barnabas* RE Day. Having only joined the *Barnabas* team in September 2007, these days are still quite new to me and I am only just getting to the point of having led each of the packages available at least once.

One of the notable aspects of leading these days across the country is that we rarely get two identical or even very similar experiences, as the children's responses vary considerably. This keeps us, the *Barnabas* team, on our toes and also allows us the opportunity to learn from the children and adapt what we do as a result.

Often we get the chance to start the day in school by leading collective worship—possibly more well-known as 'assembly'. This gives the school the chance to meet us, to discover what the day might be about, and to begin to experience the creative ways used to explore a theme. Throughout the day, we will usually work with various class sizes, covering children aged from 4 to 11 years.

Children are often very good at expressing their thoughts and feelings and it is a privilege when they share those responses with us during the day. It is encouraging when a child comes to us at the end of a session with words such as 'fab, brill, ace, cool, wicked'—all of which mean that they have enjoyed their time! For me personally, though, it is when a child shares their insight into faith, or says something about the faith journey that they are on, that we receive the greatest sense of encouragement and inspiration for what we do in *Barnabas*.

You may be asking, 'How can I help with this ministry?' I know that many of you pray for the *Barnabas* team, and we very much appreciate your prayers. RE Days are great but they can be very tiring. The journey to and from a school is sometimes smooth and pleasurable but, at times, it can be long and frustrating, with much of the journey taking place in the early hours. We value your prayers for safety as we travel, and for the energy and creativity needed to offer the very best that we can to the staff and children with whom we are working in school.

Please do also pray for the people in the *Barnabas* RE Day freelance team who take on bookings if Lucy, Martyn, Chris or Jane cannot do a requested date. The people within this team are based around the country and, between them, have many gifts including music, drama, dance and mime. We are very grateful to them for their input and for their willingness to be a part of this work. The team is growing in number, and we would appreciate your prayers that the Lord would guide us as we decide when it might be appropriate to expand the team further in specific areas of the country.

We value your prayers for safety as we travel

Maybe you feel you are not able to be involved in a practical way with your local schools, but perhaps you could consider praying for them—the children, staff and governors. Some may have parents' prayer groups that would appreciate your involvement, or it might be possible for you to have a map of the local area at home, using it to pray for children in certain roads or areas at different times.

Maybe you do feel you would like to be practically involved in the school, but are not sure how. Many schools offer a number of opportunities for people to help. There are certain legal requirements that the school needs to fulfil, in order for you to take part, but schools are usually only too happy to have support and help from others.

Some schools have a system whereby adults go into school to listen to individual children read. Some may have a 'buddy' scheme in which an adult will go in to support a child who has particular needs. Perhaps you could consider helping one lunchtime a week, or when a school is putting on a specific event, such as a school fair. All of these occasions offer opportunities to support and encourage the life of your local school.

Children offer a great deal to us and we can benefit and learn from our relationships with them. That in itself is an encouragement to invest in those relationships, but maybe more significant are the words of Jesus himself in Luke 9:48: Then Jesus said to them, 'Whoever welcomes this little child in my name welcomes me; and whoever welcomes me welcomes the one who sent me. For whoever is least among you all is the greatest' (TNIV).

Jane Butcher is a trained teacher and children's worker. Along with Lucy Moore, Martyn Payne and Chris Hudson, she is a key member of the Barnabas *ministry team.*

Mentoring others

Tony Horsfall

Spiritual mentoring is a contemporary way of describing the ancient Christian practice of spiritual direction. The main aim is to help another person to become aware of and respond to the activity of God in their life. It involves prayerful listening, with a minimum of advice-giving: the mentor is simply helping the mentoree to discern for themselves what God is doing or saying. It is a releasing, empowering ministry.

Most of us are familiar with the image of the Christian life as a journey. Spiritual mentoring is about accompanying people on that journey, helping them to see the way ahead and to avoid any pitfalls or dangers. Throughout my own spiritual journey I have benefited enormously from trusted 'guides' who have come alongside me at crucial moments in my life, often informally, sometimes in a more intentional way. I consider it an enormous privilege now to offer this kind of accompaniment to others, whether in a formal training context, the less formal setting of a retreat, or on a one-to-one basis.

For the last few years I have been leading a mentoring programme in Singapore. This tiny island state has a population of about 4 million and is modern, progressive and sophisticated. Churches are flourishing, but some congregations appear very 'driven'. This, coupled with the frantic pace of life, has resulted in lots of believers exploring a more contemplative approach, seeking a deeper reflective walk with God.

I developed the mentoring programme to meet this need. There are six modules, taken over a two-year period. Each module centres on a chosen text, with a written assignment based on what has been read, and then a tutorial with myself, followed by a Quiet Day or Retreat on the same theme. Each module is designed to help the participants build their inner life and prepare them to help others to do the same. We cover themes such as intimacy with God, knowing our identity as God's beloved children, how to abide in Christ, and how to become a soul friend. The group dynamic is very much part of the process, as is the opportunity for individual time with me. We have just over 20 in the present group from a wide range of churches, including missionaries, church leaders and active lay people.

We are currently reading *The Return of the Prodigal Son* by Henri Nouwen, the chosen text for the second module about our identity in Christ. I continually find (and know from personal experience) that the real challenge is to get the truth of our belovedness from our heads to our hearts. The combination of reading, reflection, group interaction and devotional retreat seems to be effective in helping this movement to take place.

Celtic Christians used to say that a person without a soul friend or guide was like a body without a head. Many people nowadays are discovering for themselves the advantages of having a mentor. Spiritual mentoring enables us to grow as disciples without having to fit into a prepackaged mould. It respects individuality yet holds us accountable for growth and development. This flexibility of approach is well suited to a postmodern world and has much to offer the Church today.

My work as a retreat leader brings me into contact with many such individuals. I find that once people step aside from their everyday concerns in order to focus on their relationship with God, and have unhurried time to relax and reflect, spiritual formation becomes much more natural and attainable. I continue to be amazed at the importance of 'holy listening' as part of this process. Once individuals feel safe and respected, and know they can open themselves up in the context of loving acceptance, real progress can be made in allowing God to do that deeper work in their lives.

Often I will journey alongside people simply for the time of retreat. We may follow up with an exchange of emails afterwards, but often geography will keep us from developing an ongoing relationship. Occasionally, a more long-term connection is made with someone who lives nearby and we can meet more regularly. This meeting may be to talk about specific issues (groans), to explore the way ahead (guidance) or to help someone draw closer to God (growth).

There is currently a great need to develop spiritual mentors who can help others to grow in Christ—people who have a real experience of God themselves, are good listeners, and have the wisdom that comes from knowing scripture and having lived a bit. They must be humble and self-aware, have a genuine love for others and be able to keep confidences. Above all, they must be dependent upon God, in tune with the Holy Spirit, and of a prayerful disposition.

Tony Horsfall is a freelance training consultant and retreat leader, and is the author of Mentoring for Spiritual Growth *(BRF, 2008). His website can be found at www.charistraining.co.uk. To order a copy of* Mentoring for Spiritual Growth, *see page 159.*

The Bible Reading Fellowship
15 The Chambers, Vineyard, Abingdon OX14 3FE, United Kingdom
Tel: 01865 319700; Fax: 01865 319701
E-mail: enquiries@brf.org.uk
Website: www.brf.org.uk

ISBN 978 1 84101 515 6

Distributed in Australia by:
Willow Connection, PO Box 288, Brookvale, NSW 2100.
Tel: 02 9948 3957; Fax: 02 9948 8153;
E-mail: info@willowconnection.com.au
Available also from all good Christian bookshops in Australia.
For individual and group subscriptions in Australia:
Mrs Rosemary Morrall, PO Box W35, Wanniassa, ACT 2903.

Distributed in New Zealand by:
Scripture Union Wholesale, PO Box 760, Wellington
Tel: 04 385 0421; Fax: 04 384 3990; E-mail: suwholesale@clear.net.nz

Distributed in Canada by:
The Anglican Book Centre, 80 Hayden Street, Toronto, Ontario, M4Y 3G2
Tel: 001 416 924-1332; Fax: 001 416 924-2760;
E-mail: abc@anglicanbookcentre.com; Website: www.anglicanbookcentre.com

Publications distributed to more than 60 countries

Acknowledgments
The New Revised Standard Version of the Bible, Anglicized Edition, copyright © 1989, 1995 by the Division of Christian Education of the National Council of the Churches of Christ in the USA. Used by permission. All rights reserved.

The Holy Bible, New International Version, copyright © 1973, 1978, 1984 by International Bible Society. Used by permission of Hodder & Stoughton Limited. All rights reserved. 'NIV' is a registered trademark of International Bible Society. UK trademark number 1448790.

The New Jerusalem Bible, published and copyright © 1985 by Darton, Longman and Todd Ltd and les Editions du Cerf, and by Doubleday, a division of Bantam Doubleday Dell Publishing Group, Inc. Used by permission of Darton, Longman and Todd Ltd, and Doubleday, a division of Random House Inc.

Extract from 'Inspired by love and anger': words John L. Bell and Graham Maule © WGRG, Iona Community, Glasgow G2 3DH. Used with permission.

Extract from 'Heaven shall not wait': words John L. Bell and Graham Maule © WGRG, Iona Community, Glasgow G2 3DH. Used with permission.

Printed in Singapore by Craft Print International Ltd

SUPPORTING BRF'S MINISTRY

BRF is a Christian charity committed to resourcing the spiritual journey of adults and children alike. For adults, BRF publishes Bible reading notes and books and offers an annual programme of quiet days and retreats. Under its children's imprint *Barnabas*, BRF publishes a wide range of books for those working with children under 11 in school, church and home. BRF's *Barnabas Ministry* team offers INSET sessions for primary teachers, training for children's leaders in church, quiet days, and a range of events to enable children themselves to engage with the Bible and its message.

We need your help if we are to make a real impact on the local church and community. In an increasingly secular world people need even more help with their Bible reading, their prayer and their discipleship. We can do something about this, but our resources are limited. With your help, if we all do a little, together we can make a huge difference.

How can you help?

- You could support BRF's ministry with a donation or standing order (using the response form overleaf).

- You could consider making a bequest to BRF in your will, and so give lasting support to our work. (We have a leaflet available with more information about this, which can be requested using the form overleaf.)

- And, most important of all, you could support BRF with your prayers.

Whatever you can do or give, we thank you for your support.

BRF – resourcing your spiritual journey

BRF MINISTRY APPEAL RESPONSE FORM

Name ______________________________

Address ______________________________

______________________________ Postcode ______________

Telephone ______________ Email ______________________

(tick as appropriate)

Gift Aid Declaration

☐ I am a UK taxpayer. I want BRF to treat as Gift Aid Donations all donations I make from 6 April 2000 until I notify you otherwise.

Signature ______________________________ Date ______________

☐ I would like to support BRF's ministry with a regular donation by standing order (please complete the Banker's Order below).

Standing Order – Banker's Order

To the Manager, Name of Bank/Building Society ______________________

Address ______________________________

______________________________ Postcode ______________

Sort Code ______________ Account Name ______________________

Account No ______________________________

Please pay Royal Bank of Scotland plc, London Drummonds Branch, 49 Charing Cross, London SW1A 2DX (Sort Code 16-00-38), for the account of BRF A/C No. 00774151

The sum of ______ pounds on ___ /___ /___ (insert date your standing order starts) and thereafter the same amount on the same day of each month until further notice.

Signature ______________________________ Date ______________

Single donation

☐ I enclose my cheque/credit card/Switch card details for a donation of

£5 £10 £25 £50 £100 £250 (other) £ ______ to support BRF's ministry

Credit/ Switch card no. ☐☐☐☐☐☐☐☐☐☐☐☐☐☐☐☐☐☐☐☐☐☐

Expires ☐☐ ☐☐ Issue no. of Switch card ☐☐☐

Signature ______________________________ Date ______________

(Where appropriate, on receipt of your donation, we will send you a Gift Aid form)

☐ Please send me information about making a bequest to BRF in my will.

Please detach and send this completed form to: Richard Fisher, BRF, 15 The Chambers, Vineyard, Abingdon OX14 3FE. BRF is a Registered Charity (No.233280)

Please note our subscription rates 2009–2010. From the May 2009 issue, the new subscription rates will be:

Individual subscriptions covering 3 issues for under 5 copies, payable in advance (including postage and packing):

			UK	SURFACE	AIRMAIL
GUIDELINES	each set of 3 p.a.		£13.80	£15.00	£17.10
GUIDELINES	3-year sub	i.e. 9 issues	£33.00	N/A	N/A

Group subscriptions covering 3 issues for 5 copies or more, sent to ONE address (post free):

GUIDELINES	£11.10	each set of 3 p.a.

Please note that the annual billing period for Group Subscriptions runs from 1 May to 30 April.

Copies of the notes may also be obtained from Christian bookshops:

GUIDELINES	£3.70 each copy

SUBSCRIPTIONS

❑ Please send me a Bible reading resources pack to encourage Bible reading in my church

❑ I would like to take out a subscription myself (complete your name and address details only once)

❑ I would like to give a gift subscription (please complete both name and address sections below)

Your name ____________________

Your address ____________________

____________________ Postcode ____________

Gift subscription name ____________________

Gift subscription address ____________________

____________________ Postcode ____________

Please send *Guidelines* beginning with the May / September 2009 / January 2010 issue: (delete as applicable)

(please tick box)	UK	SURFACE	AIR MAIL
GUIDELINES	❑ £13.80	❑ £15.00	❑ £17.10
GUIDELINES 3-year sub	❑ £33.00		

I would like to take out an annual subscription to *Quiet Spaces* beginning with the next available issue:

(please tick box)	UK	SURFACE	AIR MAIL
QUIET SPACES	❑ £16.95	❑ £18.45	❑ £20.85

Please complete the payment details below and send your coupon, with appropriate payment, to:

BRF, 15 The Chambers, Vineyard, Abingdon OX14 3FE.

Total enclosed £ ____________ (cheques should be made payable to 'BRF')

Payment by cheque ❑ postal order ❑ Visa ❑ Mastercard ❑ Switch ❑

Card number: ☐☐☐☐☐☐☐☐☐☐☐☐☐☐☐☐

Expires: ☐☐☐☐ Security code ☐☐☐ Issue no (Switch): ☐☐☐☐

Signature (essential if paying by credit/Switch card) ____________________

BRF is a Registered Charity

BRF PUBLICATIONS ORDER FORM

Please ensure that you complete and send off both sides of this order form.

Please send me the following book(s):

		Quantity	Price	Total
569 9	Fasting and Feasting *(G. Giles)*	____	£7.99	____
546 0	Creative Ideas for Quiet Corners *(L. Chambers)*	____	£6.99	____
587 3	Into Your Hands *(K. Scully)*	____	£6.99	____
575 0	Growing Women Leaders *(R. Ward)*	____	£8.99	____
533 0	Creative Communion *(M. Withers)*	____	£7.99	____
562 0	Mentoring for Spiritual Growth *(T. Horsfall)*	____	£7.99	____
030 4	PBC: 1 & 2 Samuel *(H. Mowvley)*	____	£7.99	____
028 1	PBC: Nahum to Malachi *(G Emmerson)*	____	£7.99	____
191 2	PBC: Matthew *(J. Proctor)*	____	£8.99	____
047 2	PBC: Ephesians to Colossians and Philemon *(M. Maxwell)*	____	£7.99	____

Total cost of books £ ________

Donation £ ________

Postage and packing £ ________

TOTAL £ ________

POSTAGE AND PACKING CHARGES				
order value	UK	Europe	Surface	Air Mail
£7.00 & under	£1.25	£3.00	£3.50	£5.50
£7.01–£30.00	£2.25	£5.50	£6.50	£10.00
Over £30.00	free	prices on request		

See over for payment details. All prices are correct at time of going to press, are subject to the prevailing rate of VAT and may be subject to change without prior warning.

PAYMENT DETAILS

Please complete the payment details below and send with appropriate payment and completed order form to:

BRF, 15 The Chambers, Vineyard, Abingdon OX14 3FE

Name ______________________________

Address ______________________________

____

______________________________ Postcode ____________

Telephone ______________________________

Email ______________________________

Total enclosed £ _________(cheques should be made payable to 'BRF')

Payment by cheque ❏ postal order ❏ Visa ❏ Mastercard ❏ Switch ❏

Card number: | | | | | | | | | | | | | | | | |

Expires: | | | | | Security code | | | | Issue no (Switch only): | | | | |

Signature (essential if paying by credit/Switch card)______________________

❏ Please do not send me further information about BRF publications.

ALTERNATIVE WAYS TO ORDER

Christian bookshops: All good Christian bookshops stock BRF publications. For your nearest stockist, please contact BRF.

Telephone: The BRF office is open between 09.15 and 17.30. To place your order, phone 01865 319700; fax 01865 319701.

Web: Visit www.brf.org.uk

BRF is a Registered Charity